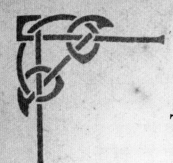

THE WORLD OF

V I K  N G S ™

by JUSTIN POLLARD
foreword by MICHAEL HIRST

CHRONICLE BOOKS
SAN FRANCISCO

For Steph, Coco, and Fliss.
Jafnan er hálfsögð saga ef einn segir.
–JUSTIN POLLARD

For my mentor and friend, Nicolas Roeg.
–MICHAEL HIRST

MGM Consumer Products would like to thank the following people for their invaluable efforts in the making of this book: Michael Hirst, Justin Pollard, Roma Khanna, Steve Stark, Steve Wakefield, Sarah Malarkey, Mirabelle Korn, Ken Girotti, Joan Bergin, Tom Conroy, Mark Geraghty, Dorothy McDonnell, Susan O'Connor Cave and Aisling O'Callaghan, Bill Halliday, Dominic Remane, Lisa Clapperton, Mike Borrett, Kelly Knauff; and a special thanks to the cast and crew of *Vikings* for their time, energy and support.

Photo credits: Jonathan Hession, Bernard Walsh

www.mgm.com

Library of Congress Cataloging-in-Publication Data

Pollard, Justin, 1968-
The world of Vikings / Justin Pollard ; foreword by Michael Hirst. pages cm
ISBN 978-1-4521-4545-7 (alk. paper)
1. Vikings (Television program) I. Title.PN1992.77.V55P65 2015791.45'72--dc232015006270

Manufactured in China

MIX
Paper from
responsible sources
FSC™ C104723

Designed by Ryan Corey for Smog Design, Inc.

10 9 8 7 6 5 4 3 2 1

Chronicle Books LLC
680 Second Street | San Francisco, California 94107 | www.chroniclebooks.com

ABOVE: Siegfried (Greg Orvis) relaxes with his prosthetic head and nemesis Count Odo (Owen Roe) in a break during film making.

CONTENTS

FOREWORD

By Michael Hirst

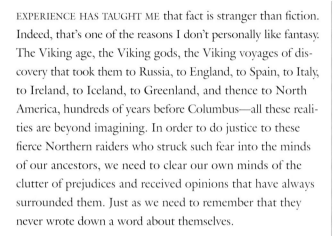

EXPERIENCE HAS TAUGHT ME that fact is stranger than fiction. Indeed, that's one of the reasons I don't personally like fantasy. The Viking age, the Viking gods, the Viking voyages of discovery that took them to Russia, to England, to Spain, to Italy, to Ireland, to Iceland, to Greenland, and thence to North America, hundreds of years before Columbus—all these realities are beyond imagining. In order to do justice to these fierce Northern raiders who struck such fear into the minds of our ancestors, we need to clear our own minds of the clutter of prejudices and received opinions that have always surrounded them. Just as we need to remember that they never wrote down a word about themselves.

The first thing I need to say about my own work on *Vikings* is that it is drama and not documentary. The second, and equally important, thing to note is that the drama is based on historical research and historical record. These two ideas are not, as some might think, contradictory. Long before I start to write, I spend weeks, even months, rummaging about in accounts of Viking life, society, and culture, teasing out story lines and watching as various characters begin to emerge from the material and claim my attention. In this process I'm helped by our historical adviser, Justin Pollard, an expert on the Dark Ages. Justin carefully guides me through the labyrinth of Viking myth, legend, and historical account so that I know my narrative is as credible and as authentic as I can make it.

Vikings have always been the "other." They have always—from the eighth century to our own—personified the threat of arbitrary and excessive violence. Appearing out of the blue, in their sleek ships with dragon heads, they fell upon poor Christian communities with brutal savagery, motivated only by greed and lust. So, anyway, the first witnesses to these events put them on record. But these scribes were Christian monks, who had every reason to spread fear about such wanton, ruthless, immoral, Iron Age pagans. What they didn't mention, because they didn't know, was that Viking society was far more open and democratic than their own. And that the Vikings had a deeper respect for women, who could own property, divorce their husbands, fight beside their brothers and sons in the shield wall, and even rule.

These things were news to me too. I don't write for educational purposes—once again, I insist that I write drama. Nevertheless, I am thrilled when what I write and produce inspires teachers and students around the world to go back to their texts and rediscover a very different Viking world. An infinitely more "real" Viking world.

I first encountered these formidable Northmen when, after writing *Elizabeth*, I was commissioned to write a movie about another famous English monarch, Alfred the Great. By Alfred's time, Viking war bands and armies were frequent visitors to the shores of Britain. Indeed, Alfred was driven out of his own kingdom of Wessex by Vikings from Denmark, who established what was called the "Danelaw" in its place. I became fascinated by these northern raiders, but quickly discovered that, since this happened during the Dark Ages, not a great deal was known about them. In any case, at the time, there did not seem to be a huge appetite to find out. Nobody, back in 1998, got excited about the Vikings.

Yet it was very different when, in 2010, MGM asked me if I was interested in writing a television drama series about them. It seemed as if everyone were suddenly interested in the subject; Vikings were in the zeitgeist, and there was talk about Viking exhibitions opening at the British Museum and all around the world.

How to account for this new interest, or the fact that the show is now being watched in 152 countries? Well, it seems that the Earth continues to deliver up new and exciting evidence of Viking presence around the globe: a second possible settlement in Nova Scotia, the frozen remains of a bejeweled Viking "princess" in Russia, a wonderful Viking hoard with precious pottery in the UK. All this is proof, if proof were needed, that the Vikings went everywhere, and that their DNA is present from the Urals to Africa.

But perhaps even more important is a new and urgent interest in paganism and Viking religion. We live in an age of religious fundamentalism—an age of conflict between absolute faiths. In the eighth century it was the same, except that the

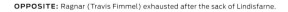

OPPOSITE: Ragnar (Travis Fimmel) exhausted after the sack of Lindisfarne.

conflict was between the Hammer and the Cross: paganism and Christianity. I always wanted to write about this subject. As a storyteller myself, I have always found the Norse sagas to be an unending source of drama. And, once again, the truth is always stranger than fiction.

My problem was: how to introduce a contemporary audience into this world? And the answer was a character called Athelstan. A young monk captured during the Vikings' first raid on mainland Britain, Athelstan began life as a device—a guide into a past and lost culture—who quickly became a character and then a living person. This is the beauty of writing a television series rather than a movie. You have time and opportunity to develop and explore all your major characters. They come alive and urge their reality upon you.

Athelstan, played brilliantly by George Blagden, is both real and fictional: a character in spiritual crisis, caught between two gods, two sets of religious beliefs. His dilemma is at the heart of the show, and I was thrilled when an article in the *Huffington Post* said that *Vikings* is "one of the few mainstream shows to take religious belief seriously."

Vikings takes other things seriously too, of course: life and death, family life, what it means to rule—but the question of faith, of spiritual life, remains central. The Vikings were the last pagans. The Viking age ended when all the countries of Scandinavia were converted to Christianity. A church was built on the ruins of the great pagan temple at Uppsala in Sweden, with its huge carvings of the gods and the folk memories of human sacrifice.

The show does not judge whether that ending was a good or bad thing. It simply attempts to dramatize, to understand, to move inside the skin of people from a different time, people who can still talk directly to ours.

—MH

ABOVE: Athelstan (George Blagden) considers if the pen really is mightier than the sword.

INTRODUCTION

A scowling horde of ghosts draws near and scurries furiously through the wind, bellowing drearily to the stars.

—Saxo Grammaticus

THE VIKINGS BELIEVED that the end of the world would occur when the god Loki escaped his chains and, with his children, Jörmungandr and Fenrir, joined the giants in attacking the gods in Asgard. During this battle, known as Ragnarök, the human heroes whom the god Odin had gathered in Valhalla would fight with him, but lose. The battle would ultimately result in the death of Odin and of many of the other gods. At the end, the sun would be extinguished and the stars would fall down. The world would then sink beneath the waves, only to emerge later, renewed.

The Christians of Europe also had a story about the end of the world, as told in two books of the Bible. The Book of Revelation describes the actual last days, but it was the Old Testament prophet Jeremiah—the weeping prophet—who identified the agents of the apocalypse when he wrote: "Out of the north an evil shall break forth upon all the inhabitants of the land."

In Europe in the early ninth century, there was little doubt in the minds of many that this prophecy had come true, and that the Vikings were the agents of the catastrophe.

Our task in making the television series *Vikings* has been to take these strange and wonderful beliefs and weave them into what we know from history and archaeology of this distant and neglected era. We wanted to place the semi-mythological heroes of the sagas into a visceral, real, early Viking world. There, we hoped, a modern audience might begin to understand what drove the Vikings out of their homelands and onto the world stage, eventually reaching from the court of Constantinople to the shores of North America.

This endeavor is made harder by the fragmentary evidence that survives. There are no great contemporary histories of the period, just a few documents written by monks. These often consist of just very brief year-by-year accounts of events as they knew them. They were certainly not "history" in the modern sense. The fuller, more colorful tales of the sagas were written long after the time in which their heroes lived, and their purpose wasn't to record history but to tell a wonderful story. No contemporary Viking accounts at all survive from this time, and the Christian chroniclers—not surprisingly—have little good to say about the Vikings. For a more in-depth look at the specific historical documents we used, please see "Sources," following.

What we have tried to do in *Vikings* is to combine the mythology and history to describe an authentic time and place, re-creating the material world based on the archaeology and contemporary descriptions available, and to fill this stage with characters imbued with the mythology of the era. In telling the tale of Ragnar and his sons, we have combined history with folklore. We have tried to create a physical world largely as it was and also to present a view of that world through the eyes of those long-ago men and women who were so steeped in story and legend.

This is a ninth century where we really can believe there are dragons and demons and Valkyries, a place where the forces of the supernatural seem all around us, just out of our sight, behind the breathtaking vistas of the real Viking age.

—JP

SOURCES

Our sources for the history of the eighth and ninth centuries are incomplete and very biased, as we have no Viking accounts from this period at all.

The history of this era comes down to us via Christian sources. These are of several types: First, there are the chronicles and annals, year-by-year accounts of events, usually written in a monastery. They are often very brief; a whole year may be recorded in a single sentence. Then there are books describing the lives of important individuals, which provide more details, such as Asser's history of Alfred the Great or Einhard's book on Charlemagne. Most of these tales, or *gestae*, are religious and take saints as their theme. Some are formed into larger "histories" that attempt to explain the growth of countries and the spread of Christianity. As their writers are usually keen to praise their subjects, they are not always the most impartial of sources. In addition, there are some administrative documents from this era, including laws, charters granting land and rights, and even some personal letters among heads of state and religious authorities, notably the Pope. We also have a few travelers' tales—accounts by Christian and Arab merchants and diplomats who recorded customs among the people they visited; their views are informed by their own ideas and prejudices. Finally, there are some artistic works consisting of stories, such as *Beowulf* and *The Battle of Maldon*, and other poetry, magical charms, and even riddles.

To hear the *authentic* voice of Vikings, we must look to the period of our television series and turn to accounts that may owe as much to legend as to fact. These are the Norse sagas and short stories, or *þáttir* , composed between the twelfth and fourteenth centuries. They deal with the history of kings and early bishops of Scandinavia, the voyages of heroes, the tales of the settlers of Iceland and Greenland, and the legends of the gods.

Aside from the sagas, there is a body of Old Norse poetry that, while written down in the twelfth century and later, may originate in earlier times—when poems were learned by heart and passed on orally from generation to generation.

The fact that our major sources for Viking history are later does not mean that the Vikings of the eighth and ninth centuries were necessarily illiterate, however. Viking runic inscriptions can be found on carved rune stones in Scandinavia and in lands visited by the Vikings, along with some graffiti, notably in the Hagia Sophia in Istanbul. Much of what Vikings from our period wrote on a day-to-day basis was probably, however, carved on wooden slips or in wax tablets and has not survived in the archaeological record.

SELECT PRIMARY SOURCES

Below are some of the primary sources and collections of primary sources that we've used for *Vikings*. It includes the contemporary annals and chronicles, as well as later sagas that provide evidence for lifestyle and culture.

SAGAS, TALES, AND EARLY VIKING HISTORIES

Ragnars saga Loðbrókar (The Saga of Ragnar Lodbrok)
Ragnarssona þáttr (The Tale of Ragnar's Sons)
Bragi Boddason, Ragnarsdrápa (Ragnar's Poem)
Krákumál (The Lay of Kraka)
Íslendingasögur (The Saga of the Icelanders)
Grænlendinga saga (The Saga of the Greenlanders)
Eiríks saga rauða ((The Saga of Erik the Red)
Bollaþáttur Bollasonar (The Tale of Bolli Bollason)
Hrólfs saga kraka (The Saga of King Hrolf Kraki)
Ynglinga Saga (The Saga of the Ynglings)
Völsunga Saga (Saga of the Völsungs)
Nibelungenlied (The Song of the Nibelungs)
Færeyinga Saga (The Saga of the Faroese)
Rauðúlfs þáttr (Rauðúlf's Tale)
Landnámabók (The Book of Settlements)
Íslendingabók (The Book of Icelanders)
Poetic Edda (a collection of Old Norse poetry from the
     manuscript known as the Codex Regius)
Snorri Sturluson, Heimskringla (The Circle of the World)
Snorri Sturluson, Prose Edda
     (An Old Norse compilation of stories)
Saxo Grammaticus, Gesta Danorum (The Deeds of the Danes)
Chronicon Roskildense (The Roskilde Chronicle)

European Chroniclers and Annalists

Adam of Bremen, Gesta Hammaburgensis Ecclesiae Pontificum
   (The Deeds of the Bishops of Hamburg)

Venerable Bede, Historia ecclesiastica gentis Anglorum
   (The Ecclesiastical History of the English people)

Abbo the Crooked, Bella Parisiacae Urbis
   (The Wars of the City of Paris)

Aethelweard , Chronicon (Chronicle)

Anglo-Saxon Chronicle

Annales Bertiniani (The Annals of St. Bertin)

Annales Cambriae(The Annals of Wales)

Annales Fuldenses (The Annals of Fulda)

Annales regni Francorum(The Royal Frankish Annals)

Annála Uladh(The Annals of Ulster)

Annales Xantenses(The Annals of Xanten)

Dudo of St. Quentin, Gesta Normannorum
   (The Deeds of the Normans)

Grandes Chroniques de France (The Great Chronicle of France)

Rimbert, Vita Ansgari (Life of Ansgar)

Other European Sources

Codex Exoniensis (The Exeter Book) which includes
   95 riddles, the poems Christ I, II, III, The Wanderer,
   The Seafarer, Widsith, The Fortunes of Men, Deor, Wulf
   and Eadwacer, The Wife's Lament, The Husband's
   Message, and The Ruin

Musica Enchiriadis (Musical handbook)

The Planctus for William Longsword
   (The Mourning for William Longsword)

Venerable Bede, De temporum ratione (The reckoning of Time)

Liber Psalmorum: The West-Saxon Psalms

"The Limousin Astronomer," Vita Hludowici Imperatoris
   (The Life of the Emperor Louis)

Thegan of Trier, Gesta Hludowici Imperatoris
   (The Deeds of the Emperor Louis)

Einhard, Vita Karoli Magni (The Life of Charlemagne)

Asser, Vita Ælfredi regis Angul Saxonum
   (The Life of Alfred, King of the Anglo-Saxons)

The West Saxon Charters of King Æthelwulf and His Sons

The Ventures of Ohthere and Wulfstan
   (recorded in the Old English text of Paulus Orosius,
   Historiae Adversus Paganos Libri VII)

Abbo of Fleury, Passio Sancti Eadmundi
   (The Passion of St. Edmund)

Gildas the Wise, De Excidio et Conquestu Britanniae
   (On the Ruin and Conquest of Britain)

Ahmad ibn Fadlān ibn al-Abbās ibn Rāšid ibn Hammād,
   Risala (Letter)

Anglo-Saxon poems from various manuscripts,
   including The Battle of Maldon, Beowulf, The Dream of
   the Rood, Caedmon's Hymn, Bede's Death Song,
   The Harrowing of Hell, and The Battle of Brunanburh.

Classical Sources

Boethius, De Consolatione Philosophiae
   (The Consolation of Philosophy) (Old English text)

Julius Caesar, Commentarii de Bello Gallico
   (Commentary on the Gallic Wars)

Gregory I, Regulae liber pastoralis (The Pastoral Care)
   (Old English text)

For a selection of translations of chronicles, letters, and charters from the period, see:

Whitelock, Dorothy, ed. English Historical Documents I:
   c. 500–1042. London: Eyre Methuen, 1979.

Douglas, David C., and George W.Greenaway, eds.
   English Historical Documents II: 1042–1189.
   London: Eyre Methuen, 1981.

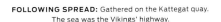

FOLLOWING SPREAD: Gathered on the Kattegat quay.
The sea was the Vikings' highway.

SOURCES 9

PART ONE:
SCANDINAVIA

VIKING SCANDINAVIA

igurd Hring had one son, who was called Ragnar. Ragnar was a big man, handsome in appearance and clever, generous with his men, but stern with his enemies. Soon after coming of age, he found himself troops and warships, and he became one of the greatest warriors, until almost no one was his match.

— SAGA OF RAGNAR

THE PEOPLE WE TODAY CALL VIKINGS had their home in the Scandinavian countries of Norway, Sweden, and Denmark. Theirs was a diverse land, covering over 300,000 square miles and stretching from the rich farming plains bordering Germany to the far north, deep inside the Arctic Circle. In the north, the land was rugged and mountainous, and in summer the sun still shone at midnight. It was a hard land to farm, and the people relied on fishing and hunting to supplement what little could be grown on the land. But if the soil was poor, the mountains, forests, and shores were rich, providing furs, amber, and walrus tusks to trade.

To the south, a more forgiving terrain allowed for extensive agriculture as well as trade with Christian neighbors and, through them, access to an extensive trade network that reached tenuously out across Russia and the Middle East, down the Silk Road as far as China. Thus, before the sea kings of the sagas, such as Ragnar, erupted onto the European stage, the earliest Vikings were farmers and traders rather than pirates and raiders.

Scandinavia at the beginning of the Viking age was not the series of discrete countries ruled by kings that it would become by the end of the period, scarcely three centuries later. The people shared a group of mutually understandable languages, which they called "the Danish tongue" and we call Old Norse. They also shared a religion. In these pagan lands, people adhered to a belief in the old Germanic gods. Never having been subsumed into the Roman empire, their ancestors had watched from outside as it waxed and waned. Emperor Constantine the Great's conversion to Christianity, and the subsequent conversion of the whole Roman empire, passed them by. Older gods still dwelled in their forests and lakes, gods who had once ruled all the Germanic lands of northern Europe but who were now confined to the remote, secluded far north.

With no contemporary Scandinavian records to help us, it is hard to be sure what turned occasional raiders into seasonal war bands and, later, into European settlers. It may be that the Norse and Danish warlords who sailed to Europe could no longer find a place for themselves in their homelands, which were coming increasingly under the control of a few powerful families. We know from a later Norwegian traveler who came to King Alfred the Great's court that his country had very limited agricultural land, confined to a narrow coastal strip, so any growth in population must have forced the weak or adventurous out to seek their fortunes elsewhere. With escalating dynastic crises in European royal families, they perhaps also saw an opportunity not simply for financial gain but for carving out new kingdoms for themselves.

By the late eighth century, only one thing was certain: The Vikings had arrived.

Ragnar Lothbrok is the first real Viking personality to emerge from the hazy accounts of this period. Even so, he belongs as much to the fable-filled pages of the sagas as to the sober entries in the chronicles of the period. Just who Ragnar was is still a matter of debate, due in part to the eagerness of contemporary writers to kill him off—an event dutifully recorded a number of times, with a number of dates, and accompanied by a number of different reasons.

The meager chronicles place him variously in England and Frankia (the territory inhabited and ruled by the people known as Franks, which would later form the core of France). By one account, he dies of dysentery at the siege of Paris; in another, he survives, only to reappear in Scotland and the Western Isles before arriving in Dublin, Ireland. An Irish tradition has him dying at the hands of rivals on Carlingford Lough, but his saga drives him on to Anglesey and then Northumbria, where he meets his nemesis, King Aelle.

That these early pirates should become folk heroes is less surprising than it might appear. The currency of the emerging Viking leaders was one we still understand today: fame. To command a great army, a Viking leader needed fame—to bring men to his side, to persuade them to follow him to danger and perhaps death, to put fear in the hearts of his enemies and rivals. Reputation made and broke Scandinavian warlords, and tales of their achievements were vital to their success. No doubt these were often greatly exaggerated even at the time, and then further embroidered with each retelling, so by the era of the saga writers such leaders had often become impossibly heroic.

Of all these heroes, the archetype was Ragnar. In fact, many who followed would be called "Sons of Ragnar," a title that was often as much a mark of honor or aspiration as a statement of genetic fact. To be a Son of Ragnar, and there were many, was to be set apart, to be a terror of the world. So successful was this family that, for generations to come, every great and powerful Norse leader would claim to be descended from the Sons of Ragnar. Their fame may still be seen in a surviving piece of Viking graffiti in the Scottish chamber tomb of Maes Howe on the Orkney Islands, which describes them as "what you would really call men."

CHAPTER
1
HOME

RAGNAR ON THE NORTH LANDS:

IT IS THE FATE OF MEN such as I to spend our days far from home in foreign lands. There is a word for it—our folk say we have gone "Viking." But why, some ask, should we leave our farms and risk our lives on the cold ocean?

The lands of the Northmen are not like the sweet meadows of the gods or even the fields of the English. Ours is a land of high mountains, of dank bogs, shimmering lakes, and dense forest. Ours is a land of barriers, where sinking marsh and towering rocks conspire with the wild animals of the woods to make each step slow and dangerous. In winter the land becomes harder still as the snow falls, and we must take to ski and skate. Then the night seems almost endless and the cold creeps around the hearth.

And so we have always lived at the edges of our land. Some grow crops in the South where the land is soft, and others hunt in the wide forests, but for many of us, the sea is our larder. It provides us with fish and seals and eggs from the birds that dwell on the cliffs. The water itself is our road. The ship is our horse and so, to us, crossing the sea has often been an easier thing than crossing the country. So perhaps we go Viking because we can. The ocean is an obstacle to our enemies, but to us it is an old friend.

There are other reasons we set forth. The world of the Christians to our south has not sat silently. The king of the Franks pushes his influence and his religion north and spreads dissent among us. We see their easy wealth and our hard living. When a man is insulted, it is only right that he should fight back.

But these are not the most powerful of reasons. A truly great man needs but one thing in life: fame. When the poets sing of a man's exploits abroad, men flock to the hero's side. He grows in strength and plans yet greater adventures. His daring brings gold to distribute to his men, and they spread glittering fame in his wake. He is then the best among them and can join the best of families, marrying his choice of women, of whom this land has precious few.

Where can a man find such fame? We learn as children that the dragon Fafnir guarded his treasure with terrible strength, breathing poison across the land. The Christians guard their gold hoard with priests and children unable to lift a sword to their own defense. Why should we not carry off what they take so little trouble to protect? It is the fate the Norns, those creatures who write our destiny, have woven for us.

This is why I cross the sea. Fame will make my name live forever. When, in time, some enemy cuts me down, the Valkyries will come and take me to Odin in Valhalla. There everyone will know my name and I will have tales to tell to the heroes of every age, as we wait in easy company for the last battle, of Ragnarök.

THE STORY OF
RAGNAR LOTHBROK

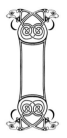

Ragnar Lothbrok is a farmer who becomes, by turns, an earl and then a Viking king. He is driven both by a desire for immortal fame and by an abiding curiosity, which he attributes to his ancestor, the god Odin. Far from the clichéd version of a Viking hero, Ragnar is thoughtful, intelligent, and introverted. He loves his sons more than plunder. He wants to pillage other lands, but he also wants to settle and farm there and become prosperous.

—MICHAEL HIRST

Ragnar Lothbrok is the first Viking to step out of Norse mythology and onto the pages of history. From his shadowy emergence until his death around AD 865, he cast a dark spell over the courts of western Europe, making the word "Viking" the ninth-century equivalent of "al-Qaeda." His journeys took him to Paris, which he sacked in 845, claiming 7,000 pounds of silver from Charles the Bald in return for not burning his capital to the ground. He also destroyed Rouen—the first appearance of the "Northmen" in what would become their land of "Normandy." But the historical Ragnar is always elusive. With never more than a brief mention in any chronicle, it is hard to be sure if all mentions even refer to the same person.

Ragnar first appears in 845. At that time, a leader of this name (or perhaps the similar-sounding "Ragnall") is recorded as leading a fleet of 120 ships up the Seine to besiege Paris. Here, in one account, his men were beset with a plague of heaven-sent dysentery and, as the chroniclers would have it, Ragnar himself succumbed, thus marking the beginning and ending of his career in one event.

The problem is that Ragnar then crops up again and again, over the next decade, prowling the seas off the coast of Scotland and the Western Isles, before apparently settling in Viking Dublin. Here he once again met his death, around 852, at the hands of other Scandinavians, either in battle or tortured to death, depending on the tale. He is recorded as dying once more at Carlingford Lough at the hands of rivals, then again during a raid on the island of Anglesey, and finally in Northumbria, where he was said to have been thrown into a pit of venomous snakes.

To put any flesh on the oft-buried bones of Ragnar, we are forced to turn to what later Scandinavian poets recorded in the *Saga of Ragnar* and the *Tale of the Sons of Ragnar*. This is the Ragnar his own descendants knew—the greatest hero of his age, who in later stories grew to become the greatest of any age. In his saga he is briefly king of Sweden and Denmark, claiming direct descent from Odin. This is a Ragnar who killed a ferocious dragon and thus won the hand of a beautiful maiden. A man whose sons became so great that he feared they would eclipse his own fame, and so he risked everything, on the expedition to Northumbria that would prove his undoing.

Ragnar is a man on the very edge of myth, part historical character, part saga hero. With Ragnar we have the best of both worlds: an epic hero who was also a real man—that essential hook that allows writers like Michael Hirst not only to tell a wonderful tale, but also to claim in hushed tones that it was a true one.

OPPOSITE: Ragnar in mourning after the murder of his friend Athelstan.
PREVIOUS SPREAD: Travis Fimmel as Ragnar Lothbrok.

TRAVIS FIMMEL (RAGNAR LOTHBROK): I think Ragnar strongly believes he is doing what is best for his people. He may be wrong, but he will do what he believes is best. Sometimes this puts a lot of strain on his relationships with those around him. When the others talk, they only talk about what's best for each of them individually, not what is best for everyone. This is a big reason why Ragnar doesn't trust anyone else to make big decisions. But he tries very hard to educate Björn to think before he acts. He believes that Björn is the only person who has what it takes to truly lead.

I believe that people who accomplish great things have a great passion and drive in them, something they've had since they were born. They are not taught, but they learn. They figure things out and always think for themselves rather than follow others like sheep. Maybe Ragnar's belief that he is a descendant of Odin is the driving force that inspires him to lead?

KATHERYN WINNICK (LAGERTHA): Ragnar and Lagertha have a long history, and their relationship has changed and evolved throughout the years. First loves always have a strong impact on you, and, for Lagertha, I feel she always has a special place in her heart for Ragnar.

CLIVE STANDEN (ROLLO): Rollo loves Ragnar and would take an ax to anyone's neck if they laid a finger on his brother. At the same time, years of sibling rivalry have taken their toll, and he believes that everything he has ever had, any chance of happiness he might have garnered, Ragnar has always taken from him, starting with Lagertha, Rollo's first and only true love.

GEORGE BLAGDEN (ATHELSTAN): The thing that connects Athelstan and Ragnar—who seem, when they meet each other, to be worlds apart—is their unshakable curiosity in the face of adversity. Each ends up being the only person in the other's world whom he can totally trust, and therefore their relationship is one of the strongest bonds of any of the characters on the show.

KARI SKOGLAND (DIRECTOR): Travis is always looking for ways as an actor to make it real, which makes my job as a director very easy. When we were out at sea, the actors were fishing between takes and proudly caught a few mackerel. Travis said to me, "It would be very realistic for us Vikings to eat these fish raw while we are doing the scene." I jokingly called his bluff and said, "Sure, I guess it's kind of like sushi—if you are game, it would be great!" Much to my surprise, he wasn't kidding. He and the other actors ate a bunch of raw fish during the scene as they head for the shores of England—very Viking!

DONAL LOGUE (KING HORIK): Travis has tremendous power when he is still. That's not because he merely looks the part of the action hero, it's because of the level of his mental vigor behind his eyes. He is great as Ragnar and delivers great, impassioned speeches—but his power is in stillness. Michael told me that in the last episode of Season 2, in which Horik is killed by Ragnar, the only words spoken by Travis the whole episode were the reciting of the Lord's Prayer with Athelstan. I couldn't believe it, even though I had journeyed with him through that episode. His performance is breathtakingly powerful. Without saying anything, he says everything.

NATHAN O'TOOLE (YOUNG BJÖRN): The funniest thing that happened during the making of the show is when Travis blocked all the dressing room doors while the other cast members were changing costumes. Travis made his way down to the set. The director and crew were waiting to shoot and Travis, being Travis, said, "What's keeping them? We haven't got all day," getting all of us into trouble when we arrived late on set.

POLL MOUSSOULIDES (DIALOGUE COACH): When Travis speaks Anglo-Saxon (also called Old English), it has to sound completely different from the natural and free-flowing Old Norse which is Ragnar's native language. One of the tricks we use is to see if there are any similar-sounding English words, which makes it easier for the actors to learn and speak. For example, in the first battle scene on the beach, one of Ragnar's lines in Anglo-Saxon is: "*Hē forþencþ þē*"—which means, "He doesn't trust you." When slightly mispronounced, this sounds remarkably like "He so sexy," and this is pretty much what Travis said. Rewind the scene and, now you know, you'll get a laugh out of it!

TRAVIS FIMMEL (RAGNAR LOTHBROK): The thing I like most about Ragnar are his flaws, his human emotion. I like how far he would go to protect his family. I don't like him when he is being lovey-dovey. It bores me to death. And I personally hate when he makes speeches to the Vikings. I hate speaking in front of groups . . . and spicy food.

ABOVE: "Out of the north an evil shall break forth upon all the inhabitants of the land." – Jeremiah (1:14)
OPPOSITE: Life behind the shield wall. Ragnar sets out to conquer the world.

VIKING FARMS

Although the Vikings burst into the pages of history as pirates and raiders, the vast majority were, in fact, farmers and traders.

Viking farms were family collectives. Children, parents, and grandparents all lived together. If the farmer kept workers, servants, or slaves, they also usually lived in the family house.

Men and boys worked in the fields, scavenged for wild food, hunted, and traveled to trade. Women prepared and preserved the food, maintained the house, fed the animals, and made the clothes. There was always a loom on the farm, and no woman ever sat idly—she was always either spinning with a spindle whorl, working on a loom, or making straps and belts by box weaving.

The Vikings grew wheat, barley, oats, and rye in small fields. Flax was also grown for making linen. Fish was an important part of the Viking diet, and they also raised pigs, cattle, sheep, goats, geese, and chickens. Sheep and goats were used mainly for milk, which could be preserved as butter and cheese. The Vikings were fond of pork and beef and also ate horse meat and goat meat, and they hunted deer for venison, as well as whales and seals.

A common meal seems to have been gruel—a porridge with whatever scraps of meat were at hand, eaten in the morning. Most joints of meat would be boiled in a cauldron rather than roasted, and were fished out with a meat hook. There are references to "cauldron snakes," which are probably boiled sausages.

The Vikings could not grow enough food to keep much livestock through the winter. So in autumn they killed many animals and salted or smoked the meat to preserve it. Vikings drank mead, a drink made from honey, water, and yeast; cider; beer; and, if they could afford it, imported wine from the Christian lands to the south.

The great danger for farmers in northern latitudes was crop failure—the growing season was very short, so a bad hailstorm could ruin the year's crop in a matter of minutes, and drought was a grave threat. If crops failed, there was no chance to plant again, no seed for next year, and nothing to eat in the winter. Every Viking was a hostage to fortune.

ABOVE: Early concept art for Ragnar's home at Kattegat.
OPPOSITE: Living off the land. Lagertha (Katheryn Winnick) and Gyda (Ruby O'Leary) fishing.

DESIGNING A VIKING VILLAGE

We know something of how Viking settlements looked from archaeological excavations. Forms varied among what are today Denmark, Sweden, and Norway, but the central element in every settlement was where the family lived—the longhouse. This essential structure accommodated not only the people but also the animals, who needed protecting from the winter weather and also provided welcome heat to the house.

For our invented settlement of Kattegat we chose wooden-walled buildings of the Danish type, as these provided more options for lighting difficult, dark interiors. We built the scale and sophistication of the settlement over time to mirror the development of the story.

TOM CONROY (PRODUCTION DESIGNER): We decided that "our" Vikings would be from southern Norway. They would inhabit a dark, gritty, chthonic world that was at the same time inspiring and sublime—still fjords, towering peaks, with the sense that nature and the supernatural were very, very close to ordinary life. I scoured the locations and found County Wicklow, just south of Dublin, which had some very unspoiled and remote-feeling countryside (an area originally called Vikinga-ló, then Wykinglo, and now Wicklow). Two very beautiful, if inaccessible, valleys were the best options for our story. I broke the bad news to the producers that road and bridge building might be necessary.

BILL HALLIDAY (VFX PRODUCER): There is still quite a bit of landscape augmentation that we do to the Irish material. It is typically done as a digital matte painting. We manipulate the Norwegian still photography into the Irish environments, often projecting the matte paintings onto a computer model to give it dimension, to allow for camera movement.

There are sometimes more than one hundred shots in a given episode—a lot by television standards. The mountains surrounding Kattegat are one great example; a lot of people wouldn't even register it, but nearly every wide-angle shot featured in the show at that location contains a partially digital background.

TOM CONROY (PRODUCTION DESIGNER): We made sketches and created reference books of the many props that

would be needed and then took these to India, where large teams of talented craftsmen in different states handcrafted all the props and dressings. Furniture, beds, and thrones were made in Jaipur, fabrics sourced in New Delhi, swords made in Agra, shields manufactured in Jhansi, and old leather pots found in Jodhpur. Eight forty-foot containers then made their way across the Indian Ocean, up through the Suez Canal, then over to Rotterdam, finally making their way to Dublin port.

Twenty thousand square feet of grass turf was purchased and encouraged to grow wild on the lot. Thousands of dried fish were sprayed with resin and hung on specially constructed "fish drying racks," a technique I has seen used by the Ainu people of northern Japan and the Russian Far East. Viking looms were reconstructed and weavers commissioned to make typical Viking patterns on them, with specially dyed wool.

Farm implements were made; outbuildings, fences, and barriers constructed. Fish traps were set up in the waters, which actually proved *too* effective—I spent one Saturday in the lake water with my nine-year-old son, Fionn, freeing all the fish! In short, every aspect of the material culture of the Vikings was researched, imagined, and re-created.

JIL TURNER (SET DECORATOR): I always knew there would be a large amount of prop making, but I never realized just how much we would have to make from scratch. From iron nails, studs, rings, and hooks to our very own Viking round-linked chain that is now evident on all the sets. Dragon heads were modeled and cast in our studio prop-making workshops. We had 140 pipe-shaped oak barrels made in Serbia

to our specification, as there were only Victorian-shaped examples available to rent. We sourced and bought from all over Europe hundreds of skulls and antlers, from deer, elk, sheep, and horse to tiny, bird-sized skulls.

Reindeer skins were sourced from Scandinavia, sheep skins from an organic tannery in England. Saxon "golden loot" came from Italian and English prop houses. Candles were commissioned from Spain to our color specifications. Wattle (woven wood) fencing came from Poland, and poles from India, and a talented local Irish blacksmith made hanging griddles for our forges and fires that are included in almost every set.

CLIVE STANDEN (ROLLO): If I could keep one prop, it would have to be the sun shadow board, or *Solskuggefjøl*, from the very first season. I'm quite sentimental. It was the one object that bonded the two brothers on their quest to go west to England. Those were the first scenes I actually shot

on the series, and it's where this crazy journey began for me and Travis. The sun shadow board and sun stone [see "Sailing and Navigation," p. 89] personify that for me.

NATHAN O'TOOLE (YOUNG BJÖRN): I actually received one of the best props I could have from the show when I finished. It's Ragnar's black-and-red shield that he used throughout the season and has all the cast and crew's signatures and messages on the back of the shield.

GUSTAF SKARSGÅRD (FLOKI): If I could keep one prop from the show? Easy, my boat!

TRAVIS FIMMEL (RAGNAR LOTHBROK): I would love to put Ragnar's boat up a tree on the farm for my niece and nephews to play in.

ABOVE: Home. A Viking-homestead interior built at Ashford studios in Ireland.

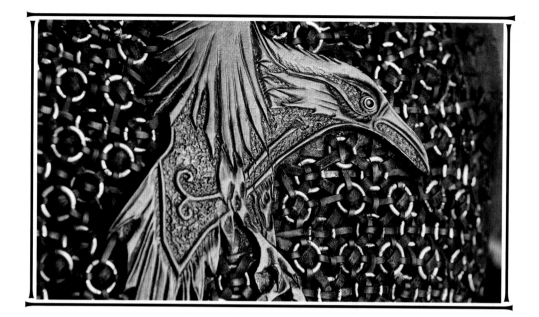

DRESSING RAGNAR LOTHBROK

Nearly everything we know of how the world of Vikings looked comes from archaeological records and later chronicles, so re-creating the image of the greatest Viking of all was an immense challenge.

JOAN BERGIN (COSTUME DESIGNER): From the beginning, the challenge was to create a look for Ragnar that signaled he was already a little different among his fellow townsmen. I have learned from experience to hold my nerve and reveal this visual character journey . . . slowly. In episodic TV there is a long road ahead. Dee Corcoran's hairstyle for Ragnar acted as a linchpin for his early costumes. Harsh, powerful, and oddly elegant. The aimed-for effect was of a compact, centered being whose clothes fit for purpose but also masked a powerful presence—and had the audience hooked from the very first episode.

DEE CORCORAN (CHIEF HAIR DESIGNER): It was important to make a statement with Ragnar. I wanted his hair to really stand out, for the audience to immediately recognize that he was a force to be reckoned with. I was really happy with the design—the hair swung and moved well in battle but was still very masculine and strong. Travis was cast with quite short hair, so we had to attach a lot of real hair extensions, which

took quite a long time. I'm pretty sure he hated every minute of putting the extensions in, but he was delighted with the finished look.

TOM MCINERNEY (CHIEF MAKEUP ARTIST): All the tattoos are taken from early Viking wood and stone carvings. We look for genuine source material before we begin the process of translating the images into tattoos. The original source material is far more beautiful than any modern interpretation of Viking artwork out there today. Depending on size, it may take up to an hour to apply a tattoo, but the actors love them.

JOAN BERGIN (COSTUME DESIGNER): The on-set ravens would eat you without salt. They took great exception to my always worn black hat, thinking, I fear, that I was in direct competition to their master Odin (Eddie the animal handler), who wore a bigger black hat than mine. I was much deflated by their undisguised animosity!

ABOVE: The magical symbol of the raven was believed to provide protection in battle.
OPPOSITE: Iron and fur – the clothes of a Viking warlord.

CHAPTER
2
ᚠᚨᛗᛁᛚᚤ

LAGERTHA ON HOME AND HEARTH:

THERE IS NOWHERE ON THIS MIDDLE EARTH more welcoming to us than the hall of our kin. This is where we belong.

The homes of the Northmen are of one kind, although of many sizes and made from many things. Kings and *jarls* (earls) build their halls in wood, joining planks tightly to make the walls, while the farmers build only the frame in wood, filling in the gaps with woven panels smeared in dung. In the far north, where wood is scarce, stones or turf are heaped up into walls, and the grassy roofs huddle under looming cliffs.

Inside, each house is familiar to all. In the middle, the hearth runs down the length of the hall. It is the hearth that provides light to the room and food to the family. Over the fire hang the iron pots in which we boil our meat. In the embers of the fire sits the griddle on which we bake our barley bread, beside the quern stone where we grind the flour. By the fire, the soapstone pots, in which we make cheese, gently warm. The fire never dies but burns always.

Down each side of the hall run earthen benches. Here the women weave by day, then smooth the cloth on whalebone boards. Here the men mend their hunting gear and prepare for expeditions. At one end of the halls stands a partition wall and beyond this are the animal stables and food stores. The northern winter is too cold and dark to leave livestock outside, so they live in the house with us; their warm bodies take the chill from the air. Outside the hall lie other buildings as each family needs. Some have a forge for mending iron tools and weapons; others have huts for smoking fish and meat. Some have places for their slaves to sleep.

But it is the hall that is the home. When night falls, the whole family gathers around the fire and passes time in games and stories. Some play games of skill such as *hnefatafl*; others try their luck with dice. Someone may strike up a tune on a bone flute or tell tales of the heroes of the past while their friends drink ale. The women sing and comb their long hair.

In the hall of a great man there is still more feasting and drinking when the traveling *skald* is invited in to recite the stories of the gods. Here the room is richly hung with tapestry, and the guests sit not on the earth but on wooden benches at tables groaning with food. All around them oil lamps light the room, their flames casting dancing shadows on the carved timbers of the roof. The men boast of their mighty ancestors and the deeds they will perform in battle, if the Norns grant them life enough. And, when the stories are told, the lord of the place brings out treasures and gives gifts to his favorites. This gold ensures the loyalty of his men. When a man has no more gold to give, his followers melt away, and his hall falls silent.

In homes great and small, when the evening is done and the fire dims, folk find a place on the benches and gather furs around them, cocooned from the cold and dark, ready to fall into the arms of sleep.

THE STORY OF
LAGERTHA

Lagertha is Ragnar's first wife and a renowned shield maiden. She continues to fight in the shield wall (the usual Viking battle formation) alongside her husband while also being a devoted mother to her son, Björn, and daughter, Gyda. Her failure to produce more sons leads to the breakup of the marriage, but Lagertha remains at the heart of the story, rising to become an earl herself, her life inextricably linked to Ragnar's.

—MICHAEL HIRST

According to the medieval Danish chronicler Saxo Grammaticus in his *Gesta Danorum* (*The Deeds of the Danes*), Ragnar's first marriage was to Lagertha, a famous shield maiden. Her career as a warrior had started when the Swedish king Frø invaded Norway, killing its ruler and placing his family and followers in a brothel to humiliate them. When Ragnar heard of the death of the king, who was his grandfather, he swore revenge and set out on an expedition to kill Frø. Hearing of his arrival, Lagertha and many other women dressed as men and joined Ragnar in battle.

During the battle, in which he killed Frø, Ragnar noted the extraordinary bravery of one woman, Lagertha, who he said had turned the battle in his favor. Vowing to marry her, he sent Lagertha messages. She appeared to respond favorably, inviting him to visit her at her house in Gaulardale. However, as a test, she set a dog and a bear at her porch to attack Ragnar when he arrived. Ragnar killed the bear with his spear and throttled the dog, and won over Lagertha to be his wife.

Later, after Ragnar divorced Lagertha, she returned to Norway. Still harboring a love for him, she came to his aid with 120 ships when Denmark descended into civil war. According to Saxo Grammaticus, at the height of the battle, Lagertha once again saved the day, as she "who had a matchless spirit though a delicate frame, covered by her splendid bravery the inclination of the soldiers to waiver."

Returning home, the victorious shield maiden decided to be ruled by men no longer and, as Saxo Grammaticus (no fan of independent women) bluntly puts it:

"[She] murdered her husband . . . in the night with a spearhead, which she had hidden in her gown. Then she usurped the whole of his name and sovereignty; for this most presumptuous dame thought it pleasanter to rule without her husband than to share the throne with him."

This mythological background proved to be the perfect starting point for our Lagertha. It allowed us to use the story elements to demonstrate the unique role of women in the real Viking world, and it provided Katheryn Winnick with the material to create a character who is match for any man and a legend in the making.

OPPOSITE: Lagertha the shield maiden.
PREVIOUS SPREAD: The family and kin groups were the heart of the Viking world.

KATHERYN WINNICK (LAGERTHA): I always viewed Lagertha as a strong individual who has had to deal with the many different challenges of being a woman. Throughout the first three seasons, Lagertha has dealt with unwanted sexual advances, losing children, infertility issues, a cheating husband, divorce, and remarrying a physically and emotionally abusive man.

Nonetheless, she has become even stronger and more independent. She has grown as a woman and as a person. I am proud to be able to play Lagertha, and if I have brought anything to the role from my own life, it is perhaps the sense of perseverance that she displays through all the challenges facing her.

In school, I was taught that women in earlier times were rarely if ever in a position of strength. Since all our history is written from the point of view of the Anglo-Saxons, it was refreshing to learn more about the actual role of Viking women—in particular, their independent spirit and ferocity when threatened.

CLIVE STANDEN (ROLLO): Lagertha and Rollo's relationship is a little complicated. She's the one that got away, the woman who left him high and dry. Even though Lagertha probably chose to leave Rollo for Ragnar, in Rollo's eyes, there is only one truth: Ragnar stole her from him.

DONAL LOGUE (KING HORIK): From the get-go, Vikings placed a heavy emphasis on powerful, enfranchised female characters—not just Lagertha, but Siggy, Porunn, and Aslaug as well. I think from the point of view of playing a male leader in a very militant culture, Horik had to have the mindset that women were not merely property (as they were seen primarily by his Frankish counterparts), but players to be taken seriously.

ABOVE: Lagertha tells Ragnar she is with child.
OPPOSITE TOP: Lagertha dreams of the world beyond the village.
OPPOSITE BOTTOM: Fate plays tricks on Lagertha with the arrival of Princess Aslaug.

DRESSING LAGERTHA

In the sagas, a shield maiden was a woman who often bore a burning grudge that could only be avenged through bloodshed, someone who put on men's clothes (somewhat taboo in Viking society) and moved into the realm of men. The purpose for us in the series was to demonstrate that women in Viking society had many more rights and freedoms than women in the rest of Europe at this date (and indeed for centuries after) and were much more vigorous actors on the public stage.

This has been borne out by recent research showing that Viking women really did have a place on the battlefield. The Byzantine chronicler John Skylitzes recorded women fighting with the Varangian Vikings (from the medieval state of Rus) against the Bulgarians in 971. Saxo Grammaticus writes that at Brávellir, where Ragnar's father and Harald Wartooth fought, it was the three hundred shield maidens who held the field. But archaeology is truly changing our view of shield maidens. For many years, a skeleton found with a sword was assumed to be a man's and one found with jewelry a woman's. Recent re-analysis of such finds in eastern England is showing that this is no more than a modern prejudice. There were women among the Viking war parties in ninth century Europe, and they were far from confined to the camp.

JOAN BERGIN (COSTUME DESIGNER): To most viewers, the fact that Lagertha is a shield maiden is of almost equal interest to her being Ragnar's wife. I started her dressed in a wool dress dyed in rich colors, with a linen underdress, and a long apron held in place by two tortoiseshell broaches, with a multicolored necklace strung between them. Her warrior clothes were rough-hewn yet sexy. Unlike Ragnar, she gradually assumes the trappings of honor, both as a mark of tradition and respect, but also because it was fascinating to keep the soldier edge to everything she wore, however splendid her later earl dresses became. We have had several requests to bring out a line of her hand-tooled leather tunics and wide belts.

DEE CORCORAN (CHIEF HAIR DESIGNER): Lagertha's hair is strong but feminine, a balance we wanted to achieve in order to represent her whole character. We wanted to ensure that her look as a shield maiden was convincing—with her hair off her face and ready for battle. But we also needed to keep her intense femininity apparent, with braiding, twists, etc. It's a badass look, and it works really well.

KATHERYN WINNICK (LAGERTHA): I strongly believe that her look, including her clothing, hair, and makeup, all help to convey her story. It's a collective process. We added more color and more metal armor as Lagertha gained status as an earl. As she gained power, her dresses became more detailed and more structured. For the warrior hairstyle, I wanted to show strength as well as practicality. Also, it was important to keep her hair soft and loose during the vulnerable and lighter scenes. Makeup is very minimal, as they wouldn't wear much day to day. I wanted to switch it and kick it up a notch for Lagertha's warrior look in Season 3. We added more black eyeliner (kohl) to create a stronger, more severe look. I figured with Lagertha having lost everything, including her earldom, I wanted to convey that she is even more fierce.

OPPOSITE: Lagertha's journey – from farmer's daughter to earl.

THE STORY OF
BJÖRN IRONSIDE

Björn is Ragnar's eldest son. Having remained unharmed in all his early battles, he earned the nickname "Björn Ironside." A fierce defender of his mother's reputation, he is also proud to be a son of Ragnar. He shares his father's abiding curiosity about other lands and other cultures—a curiosity he will in time be able to indulge.

—Michael Hirst

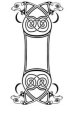

Björn Ironside is a semi-historical character recorded in several ninth-century chronicles and often said to be the first ruler of the Swedish Munsö dynasty. Most famous for his daring raid into the Mediterranean to sack medieval Luna (the modern-day site of Luni in northern Italy), he showed greater caution than many of his contemporaries, deciding to retire from raiding on his return and live out his life in wealth and ease.

According to the *Saga of Ragnar*, Björn Ironside was destined to inherit his father's kingdom in Sweden and eclipse Ragnar's memory. As Ragnar grew more jealous, he took greater risks, eventually leading to his death at the hands of King Aelle in Northumbria. Björn, along with his brothers, then took revenge on their father's killer before retiring to rule Sweden from Uppsala.

For the *Vikings* series, Björn presented both challenges and opportunities. This was a chance to see a Viking grow up, but it also meant splitting the role between two actors. Alexander Ludwig's seamless transition into the role begun by Nathan O'Toole is a testament to both actors' understanding of the character—a character with a very long journey still ahead of him.

NATHAN O'TOOLE (YOUNG BJÖRN): It was an honor to play Björn, a character to whom I bear no physical resemblance. I have brown hair and brown eyes, in comparison to Björn, who has blond hair and blue eyes. Björn's attitude is what I like most about him. Björn is fearless. He is not afraid to say what he feels and fights for what he believes in. He often comes off as rude, but he is always an honest character throughout the show.

ALEXANDER LUDWIG (ADULT BJÖRN): Björn loves his family. As they grow as a family, they become more of a unit, in that there are times when his parents have to lean on Björn. I love this dynamic and could not be more thrilled to see it grow further. In Season 3 I have a child, so I had a two-week-old baby in my arms. That was a surreal and amazing scene for me.

I know basically what my character has in store because we try to stay consistent with the historical events, but I have a lot of creative freedom to determine when and why he develops internally. It is up to Michael to determine when he fulfills his destiny, so I work with him to decide when to show certain characteristics that allude to the beginnings of Björn Ironside.

CLIVE STANDEN (ROLLO): Rollo has always been there for Björn, and very much treats him as his own, even more so when Ragnar gets swept up with his own ego and ambitions of power and he somewhat neglects his duties as a father. For Rollo, Björn is the one shining light left in Kattegat, and the information that Rollo gleans in Season 3 (that he may indeed be Björn's father) is yet another blow to him.

ABOVE: Alexander Ludwig as Björn Ironside.
OPPOSITE: A young Björn (Nathan O'Toole) enjoys a childhood on the fjords.

JOAN BERGIN (COSTUME DESIGNER): His physical aura needs costumes that show off his natural strength. The whole design of his costume is strong but simple and perfectly fitted. There is a strange challenge around designing for the next generation in what is still the ninth century! The urge is to make them a touch modern with the "cool" and urgency of youth.

DEE CORCORAN (CHIEF HAIR DESIGNER): Björn's original style was very much based on historical findings—the sharp, angular warrior cut, which is a Viking version of short back and sides and long on top. It is thought that this look originated for a few reasons. First, lice would have been a problem in those days, and, second, it was thought that it prevented an enemy grabbing the back of your head/hair in battle. As Björn's character evolves and he becomes a man in his own right, he loses the warrior cut, and we developed a shaven look with his hair knotted on top.

TRAVIS FIMMEL (RAGNAR LOTHBROK): I think one of the funniest things that happened during the making of the show is Alexander Ludwig trying to say "warriors" without an Asian accent. The poor little Canadian Wabbit.

ABOVE TOP & BOTTOM: From child to father – Björn with his mother and sister, Gyda, and later with his own child.

THE STORY OF
GYDA

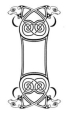
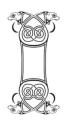

Gyda is the only daughter of Ragnar and Lagertha, and the sister of Björn. On the brink of womanhood she dies in a plague that sweeps the region and is deeply, privately mourned by her parents.

—MICHAEL HIRST

For *Vikings* we wanted to show how vital children were to Viking society, which in many ways was a world of children, as half the population was under the age of fifteen. It was your children who would look after you in old age (if you lived that long), and it was they who would keep your fame alive after your death.

This does not mean, however, that Viking children, even privileged ones such as Gyda, had an easy life. There was no formal schooling for children, and both boys and girls were expected to work as soon as they were capable of doing anything useful. Girls would be expected to spin and weave, and boys would perform the usual manual labor on a farm. Children were also regularly fostered—sent for extended stays with relatives or friends who either needed the help or had particular skills they could teach the child.

There was still time for play, and boys were encouraged to practice fighting, not simply play wrestling but single combat with weapons. Storytelling, explaining the religious mythology of the era and the history of the people, was also an important way to relax. There were some toys—dolls, model ships, balls, etc. In the Icelandic saga *Bolli Bollason's Tale*, Bolli is recorded as building himself a playhouse.

Although children were cherished, Vikings were very practical in times of stress. During famines, or when the population of an area looked to be outpacing the food supply, infants and particularly the infants of slaves, might be exposed on the mountainside in order to keep the population down.

RUBY O'LEARY (GYDA): It is exciting to imagine what life in Viking times was like. You learn about it in school and see it in books. But when you get the chance to stand on fantastic sets, surrounded by people in amazing Viking costumes, it completely brings the story to life and makes it so real. These were tough people, in very hard times, who lived lives as warriors but also had families to take care of.

My favorite scenes were with the goats. I spent free time between outdoor shoots feeding and playing with them. I had a scene where I was milking a goat and talking to Athelstan about gods but one of the goats wouldn't stay still, so they tied his rope to my stool. In the middle of a take, just as I was about to speak, the goat spooked and ran off the set, knocking me off the stool, flat onto my face! The crew found this much funnier than I did.

CHAPTER

3

PEOPLE

ROLLO ON THE FATES OF MEN:

AT NIGHT, when sleep descends across the world of men, those most hungry for fame come silently to the seer. As they look into the flames, they all ask the same question: "What is to be my fate?"

We learn that our fate lies not in the future but deep in our past. It was woven on the very night we were born, and its golden threads can never be unpicked. It was then, on our birth night, that the Norns came to our mother's house. Who are these creatures? They are many. The first three came from the land of the giants and are named *Urðr*, which means "what has happened"; *Verðandi*, meaning "what is now"; and *Skuld*, or "what must be." They came to protect the world of men, but their coming brought an end to the golden age of the gods. Now gods, too, had a fate, and with every beginning came an end.

The Norns dwell in a hall by the Well of Fate at the root of Yggdrasil, the World Tree, and their own fate is to protect the tree. Here they make the laws and lives allotted to the sons of men and set men's fates. From here the youngest, Skuld, rides with the Valkyries at Odin's command to every battle, to

decide who will live and who will die and which of the slain will join the god in Valhalla.

At this point great men look at the seer and sigh. They say, "The Norns determine the fate of men unevenly, seeing that some have a pleasant and luxurious life, while others have little fame or worldly goods; some have long life, others short. Why is this?"

This is the greatest mystery. Good men suffer evil, and evil men sometimes rejoice in the best fortune. The reason is this: The Norns are not of one kind but two. One is an honorable race whose golden yarns weave fame and good fortune, but the other is an evil caste who plait dark strands into our fate. For most of us, both will play a part at that first moment of life when our future is set.

As that moment passes, the web of fate is finished. The Norns make fast its threads in the Hall of the Moon. Now it is done and can never be undone, and the fate of that child will follow the path there written. That is the will of the Norns and the law of the world.

DESIGNING KATTEGAT

The village of Kattegat provides a central focus for the series. With each new season of production, it grows, reflecting the increasing power and status of the characters who call it home. Having started as little more than a small trading center for a number of isolated farmsteads like Ragnar's, it expands and develops with the story.

The Kattegat of *Vikings* is not based on a single actual location, as that would have limited where Michael Hirst could take the story. It is an invented settlement designed to serve as a focus and anchor point for the series. The name is a nod to the saga story in which Ragnar ruled both Sweden and Denmark, as it is the name of the sea area between the two countries. In appearance, it is based on contemporary trading settlements such as Hedeby, but its location at the head of a fjord is a reference to the description in one of the surviving copies (the "F manuscript") of the *Anglo-Saxon Chronicle* that the earliest Viking raiders came from the old Norse region of Hǫrðaland (today the Norwegian county of Hordaland).

TOM CONROY (PRODUCTION DESIGNER): We built the "seaward" side of Kattegat, our Viking town, with docks, buildings, animal pens, and fish-drying racks, on the exposed shores of Lough Tay, County Wicklow. The whole area is a nature reserve, so we anchored it all with giant removable water tanks instead of concrete foundations, as everything had to be disassembled at the end of the season.

JIL TURNER (SET DECORATOR): In Season 1, the Great Hall was Earl Haraldson's domain. I envisioned a magical place that would impress—and intimidate—the townsfolk of Kattegat when they gathered there. This earl was not a man of the people; he ruled by fear. Lighting was one of the most important features. I created these big golden dragon heads that had bowls of fire hanging from their mouths. Each upright beam has one. This gave a very dramatic effect when lit; it looked like the gods were breathing fire on all below.

By the time Ragnar became earl, I had made the whole Great Hall feel more warm and friendly. Food was cooked and distributed there, children played freely, women had their own space to make the sails for the Viking boats with their magnificent looms, and animals were brought in for the winter. Ragnar's Great Hall was a place for all of Kattegat's people, and Ragnar welcomed them all.

OPPOSITE: Conceptual artwork for the approaches to Kattegat.
PREVIOUS SPREAD: On the gimbal. Rollo and crew filming on dry land with the ship mounted on a hydraulic gimbal.

THE STORY OF
ROLLO

Ragnar's younger brother Rollo has always lived in Ragnar's shadow. Although renowned as a great warrior and as a founder of the Berserker cult, Rollo strives to be as famous as his brother, even if this sometimes means fighting against him.

—MICHAEL HIRST

The Rollo of *Vikings* is based on a historical character not in fact directly related to Ragnar but who had an equal influence in the development of the Viking world.

Rollo emerges from the *Anglo-Saxon Chronicle* in the ninth century as a Viking warlord raiding in Frankia. Norwegian and Danish historians differ as to his ancestry, but all agree that having raided along the Seine, Rollo invaded the area of northern France that became "Normandy"—the Land of the Northmen. Having forced the Frankish ruler Charles the Simple to come to terms, Rollo then consolidated his principality by converting to Christianity under the name Robert and becoming the first duke (or possibly count) of Normandy. Rollo's great-great-great-grandson William the Conqueror would invade England, finally gaining the kingship the Vikings had so long coveted.

ABOVE: Clive Standen as Rollo.
OPPOSITE: Rollo and Jarl Borg (Thorbjørn Harr) prepare for battle.

CLIVE STANDEN (ROLLO): When I was first cast in *Vikings* I had absolutely no idea quite how big a historical figure Rollo was. When I started researching and immersing myself in his world, and ultimately the world of the Vikings, I was flabbergasted to find such rich material, incredible stories of conquest, adventure, discovery, and innovation. I feel it a great privilege to be involved in bringing this culture and these fascinating—and largely misrepresented—people to the forefront of the twenty-first-century's imagination. When I read about Ragnar in the history books, he emerged as almost mythical—a legendary hero not unlike King Arthur in the Arthurian legends. By contrast, everything Rollo achieved is well documented in history; it shaped the world we live in today. His accomplishments have affected the whole of Europe and the Western world by setting up a lineage of great leaders, including William the Conqueror himself. There is a reason why his name outlived many other great Viking leaders of the time, and it's a huge honor to make him burn as brightly on the screen as he obviously did in Normandy in the year 911!

JESSALYN GILSIG (SIGGY): From Season 1, I think Siggy was attracted to Rollo physically. And maybe, if things had gone differently, it would have been an affair and nothing more. But in a time of need she saw him as a means of survival. Then, by the end of that season, she had decided to see if she could work with him as a means of building her way back into a position of power. But she and Rollo are so different. He is emotional, sentimental even. And she is rational and, in some ways, detached. There is one time in the series where they are in sync, in Season 2, when we have run from Kattegat and set up a little homestead. For a moment we are leading this small community. Because both characters are doers, they meet over the practical nature of life.

JOAN BERGIN (COSTUME DESIGNER): One has to admit that Clive, the actor, looks so good minus his top that it is tempting to leave him minus it for most of the series. However, just as the power of erotica in women's clothing is hiding then revealing, I strongly believe the same may apply to the male protagonists. Rollo's clothes need to suggest the body underneath, the struggle within his character, the anguish of what he feels is his displacement by his overly dominant brother, Ragnar.

OPPOSITE: Brothers in Arms? Strong personalities were required to lead Viking war bands and there was only room for one leader.

ROLLO THE BERSERKER

The Viking warriors known as "berserks" were the shock troops of their day. The term "berserk" itself may derive from the Old Norse for "bare of chest," implying that these troops fought that way, although some sources claim they wore wolf or bear skins, the Old Norse term being similar. Most of what we know of the berserkers comes from saga sources, so can be a bit fanciful. Their method of fighting (*berserkergang*) involved suddenly entering a terrifying state of frenzy in which they might kill anything that crossed their path. In one story (*Hrólf's Saga*), King Halfdan's berserkers are said to have killed men and cattle—or anything they came across. This obviously made them a powerful, if volatile, weapon. While they were admired in Viking society for their skill in battle, they were feared and often sidelined in peacetime.

ABOVE: Shock troops. The beserkers were the most feared of all Viking warriors.
OPPOSITE: Beserkers entered a state of frenzy that made them almost unstoppable killing machines.

THE STORY OF
SIGGY

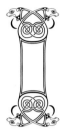

Siggy is Earl Haraldson's wife. She takes the responsibilities of ruling very seriously, and is devastated when her husband is killed. But she is also a survivor who begins a relationship with Rollo in order to prevent her expulsion by the new order. In the end she becomes indispensable to Ragnar's second wife, Queen Aslaug, helping to raise her children as well as reminding her of her duties.

—MICHAEL HIRST

Siggy takes her name from Sigyn, one of the Norse goddesses and the wife of the trickster god Loki. In the *Prose Edda*, Snorri Sturluson's thirteenth-century collection of Viking mythology, Loki's son Váli is changed into a wolf by the gods and tears apart his brother Narfi, whose entrails are then used to tie Loki to three stones. A snake is then placed above Loki; Sigyn sits beside her husband, holding a bowl to catch the venom dripping from the snake's fangs. When she goes to empty the bowl, Loki shakes furiously, eventually so much that he breaks free, ushering in the end of the world—Ragnarök.

In *Vikings* our Siggy demonstrates the mobility and dangers of Viking society, where status is defined by complex patterns of relationships and power. With Earl Haraldson alive Siggy is almost a queen, but without him her status evaporates overnight and she must rebuild her position in society from the bottom up.

JESSALYN GILSIG (SIGGY): One of the things that attracted me to *Vikings* initially was the chance to abandon preconceived ideas of women in period pieces as "the weaker sex" needing rescue. From day one, Gabriel Byrne (Earl Haraldson) and I were exploring a political marriage that was a partnership. Once Earl Haraldson was gone, the mindset stayed the same. As I wandered around the Great Hall, deposed from my throne, I watched Ragnar. Though I understood his appeal, he always seemed a novice. Everything that seemed new and exciting, all his well-intentioned ambition, read as young and naïve to me. Siggy was a watcher, gathering information, observing dynamics; she was never a romantic. Even when she was most vulnerable, after the death of the earl, she orchestrated her own rescue by killing her daughter's husband and declaring Ragnar the earl herself. She was always looking to her own survival, but I think she was also always looking for a way back to the throne, which she believed was her rightful position.

CLIVE STANDEN (ROLLO): Siggy and Rollo's relationship is a very tempestuous affair, a relationship based not on love but more on convenience. They need each other to get what they want, and I think Rollo gets confused within this agreement and starts to have genuine feelings for her. Rollo and Siggy are a powder keg waiting to explode.

DONAL LOGUE (KING HORIK): I feel like Siggy is a bit of a ninth-century Scarlett O'Hara. She does everything she has to, including things she abhors, to survive in an environment in which she is easily dispensable.

OPPOSITE: Jessalyn Gilsig as Siggy.

FIGHT TO THE DEATH

SEASON 1, EPISODE 6: "BURIAL OF THE DEAD"

Not surprisingly, there is a lot of personal combat in *Vikings*. In the ninth century, there was very little combat that wasn't personal. We hear, in poems like "The Battle of Maldon," how individuals would pick out a single warrior in an opposing army and fight one-to-one. Single combat could also prove a way of solving disputes, because in a fight it was thought that God (if you're a Christian) or the gods (if you're a Viking) would protect the right.

The idea for personal combat between Ragnar and Earl Haraldson came from an account of a Viking fight in the story of Weland, a career raider. According to the contemporary *Annals of St. Bertin*, Weland had been cornered in Frankia by Charles the Bald; to escape he used that oldest of Viking tricks, a feigned sudden conversion to Christianity. Charles believed him and even let him stay with his family at court—until two members of Weland's former war band came before the king and revealed that the conversion was fake. Weland denied it. As was the custom, one of the accusers then challenged him to mortal combat in front of King Charles. Weland was unable to refuse, the fight to the death went forward, and Weland was cut down on the spot. So ended the career of one of the greatest Vikings, at the hands of his own men.

Fight scenes in *Vikings* present a number of problems for both cast and crew. It is extremely difficult to always use stunt doubles when the action is so personal and up close. For this reason, most of the actors perform at least some of their own stunts. Many of the cast have found martial arts training to be useful. And everyone has discovered that you can never be too fit to be a Viking. Having said that, some sequences are simply too dangerous for the cast to perform, so we have a dedicated stunt team for those superhuman moments.

KATHERYN WINNICK (LAGERTHA): I have a martial arts background and hold a third-degree black belt in tae kwon do as well as a second-degree black belt in karate. What I learned above all from those disciplines is that knowledge is more powerful than physical strength. I tried to bring this quality to Lagertha in her battle sequences. She should try to outsmart her opponent and stick to her strengths as a woman—e.g., having a lower center of gravity and being quicker and smarter than her male adversaries.

CLIVE STANDEN (ROLLO): *Vikings* is a big show for stunts, and our stunt coordinators are always pushing us (as well as the budget!) with bigger and better battle choreography and exciting, death-defying stunts. Each new season is far more ambitious than the last. I love doing my own stunts; it's part of the fun and, in my opinion, makes the scene. I will probably have all sorts of joint injuries and arthritic problems

in my old age, but at least I can tell the grandkids that it was really me decimating all those Saxons on the battlefield or leaping off that castle. No one can take experiences like that away from you!

GAIA WEISS (PORUNN): When I started, no one had told me that my character was going to become a shield maiden. It was very exciting, though I was slightly nervous to fight on camera. I had never taken any martial arts class or trained my body for fighting. So, in between seasons 2 and 3, I started jeet kune do (a hybrid martial art founded by Bruce Lee in 1967) and I now go regularly to the gym.

TRAVIS FIMMEL (RAGNAR LOTHBROK): How do I prepare for the combat scenes? Easy—I have a great stunt double. His name is Franklin Henson. He does all the hard stuff for me.

ABOVE: The coup de grace. Ragnar delivers the blow that makes him earl.
OPPOSITE: Earl Haraldson (Gabriel Byrne) and Ragnar fight to the death.

AN EARL'S DEATH
SEASON 1, EPISODE 6: "BURIAL OF THE DEAD"

There is a unique document describing a Viking chieftain's funeral that we used as detailed source material for Earl Haraldson's last rites. The document, written by the tenth-century Arab traveler Ahmad ibn Fadlan, describes a funeral he witnessed among the Viking Rus (the Central European Vikings who gave their name to Russia). In this, one of the dead man's slave girls was asked to join him in the next life—to willingly become a human sacrifice. This extraordinary event provided the central theme for our funeral. It gave us a chance to mirror ibn Fadlan's amazement at this willing death, in how the Christian Athelstan in our story reacts to young Björn's explanation of what will happen.

Ibn Fadlan's account also provided us with a unique character, someone he describes as "a crone . . . whom they called the 'Angel of Death' . . . she who kills the slave girls. I myself saw her: a gloomy, corpulent woman, neither young nor old."

With an eyewitness account, we could even paraphrase some lines our source says the slave girl spoke, and put them in the mouth of our victim:

"The first time they lifted her, she said, 'Behold, I see my father and my mother.' The second time, she said, 'Behold, I see all of my dead kindred, seated.' The third time, she said, 'Behold, I see my master, seated in Paradise. Paradise is beautiful and verdant. He is accompanied by his men and his male slaves. He summons me, so bring me to him.'"

Other details, such as the slave girl having sex with men in the town before her death, allowed us to match ibn Fadlan's disgust to Athelstan's reactions, and also let Björn explain the events in a natural and apparently untroubled way.

When it came to the final send-off, it was the usual Viking custom to either burn the pyre on land or, as in the famous case of the well-preserved Viking ship found at the Oseberg farm in Norway, simply to bury the ship whole. There is no actual evidence for Vikings sending burning ships out to sea—but then there wouldn't be—however, we found inspiration in Snorri Sturluson's description of the burial of the god Baldur, whose death marks the start of events that will lead to Ragnarök.

TOM CONROY (PRODUCTION DESIGNER): One image that made a huge impression on me when I was a small boy was an illustration of a burning ship in a Viking funeral. It was quite a thrill, then, to re-create this iconic image and . . . quite a worry that we would have to risk one of our precious ships. We lined the ship with fireproof materials and made up fire-resistant dummies for Earl Haraldson and his unfortunate favorite slave. A special rig of gas burners was set up and piped to an off-camera barge holding the gas bottles.

We had enough materials for three takes. Despite some heart-stoppingly long takes, the ship survived for another day.

OPPOSITE: Earl Haraldson begins the journey to Valhalla. Note the pre-VFX landscape.
FOLLOWING SPREAD: At Uppsala, Ragnar ponders what the gods have in store.

CHAPTER
4

GODS

FLOKI ON THE GODS OF ASGARD:

LISTEN! I will tell you of the strange beings that live in Asgard.

Now, Odin sees everything that passes on earth from his high seat of Hlidskjalf in Asgard. Each night he retires to Valhalla, the Hall of the Fallen, where the great female warriors, his Valkyries, bring him the souls of brave warriors struck down in battle. In Valhalla he feeds them and gives them mead so that they will fight for him at Ragnarök, the battle at the end of the world. Here his ravens come to him each evening. They tell him of the deeds of men while he plans his battles, casting his spear down to earth to make war among men. As the night closes in, the all-seeing Odin, who sacrificed an eye at Mímir's well so that he might see the future, broods on his own coming death in the jaws of the wolf Fenrir.

With Odin sits his wife Frigg, the queen of Asgard, the mother of Baldur the Ill-fated. Her name means "love" and her home is the Marsh Hall Fensalir. She too can see our fates but never speaks of what she sees. Well she knows the ways of men and matches their brute strength with careful cunning. For this the women of Midgard hold no god in higher esteem and call to her in childbirth.

Who else walks the halls of Asgard? Happy Freyr, who rules over the rain and the shining of the sun and the fruit of the earth, who brings peace and pleasure to the realms of men. Freyr, who was not of the Aesir but of other gods, the Vanir, came to Asgard after their war. He was given the realm of the Elves as a teething gift. Freyr travels quickly over the land on the boar Gullinbursti, whose shining mane shows the path, and on the water in his ship *Skíðblaðni*, which always has a fair wind and can be folded away into a pocket. It was

Freyr who gave his sword in return for the hand of the giantess Gerðr and, for the lack of this, will die at the hand of the fire-giant Surtr at Ragnarök.

Now let me speak of Thor, whom men hold most high. It is Thor who sits in majesty at the great Temple at Uppsala, where the tree is hung with the sacrificed bodies of men and animals. Odin's child, Thor rules the sky; he governs thunder and lightning, winds and storms. With red hair and beard, Thor lives in the Field of Power in Asgard and is stronger than any. When he wears his belt, Megingjörð, his strength is doubled and the world shakes as he walks. In the iron gloves, Járngreipr, he bears his hammer, Mjöllnir, which shatters mountains and protects the Aesir from the giants.

At the end of the world, Thor will battle the World Serpent Jörmungandr and kill it, but walk just nine steps before the serpent's venom strikes him down. Then the sky will turn black, and fire will be everywhere; the stars will fall down, and water will wash over the land, until a new world rises green from the foam.

Who will bring the world to its end at Ragnarök? It is Loki, the shape-shifter, he who both helps and hinders. It was he who conspired to kill Baldur, Odin's beloved son, drawing down the wrath of the gods. But it is Loki who will be their doom. He stands now bound by the entrails of his son and causes earthquakes among men when he writhes in his bonds. Come Ragnarök, he will slip free and fight with the giants against the gods of Asgard. Loki's children will kill Odin and Thor, and the world will end. This is the fate of the gods, and this too is the fate of men.

DESIGNING THE TEMPLE

In Season 1, Episode 8, "Sacrifice," Ragnar takes his family to the Temple at Uppsala
to attend a great Viking festival. According to medieval chroniclers, Old Uppsala
(south of the modern city of Uppsala in Sweden) was the main pagan center of Sweden
and home to a great Temple dedicated to the Aesir gods. Here, every nine years,
there was a major festival during which nine of every type of male animal, including
humans, were sacrificed.

Working out what Uppsala might have looked like at this date, and more specifically what the festival was like, gave the production team a chance to fuse genuine
historical details with some truly haunting set design. The result was a scene as
powerful and shocking to a modern audience as it must have been to a first-time
visitor to the temple.

What we know of the real Uppsala is tantalizing but sparse. There are references
in the *Ynglinga Saga*, written down around 1225 by Snorri Sturleson, but our
main source is the chronicler Adam of Bremen, who describes the site in his *Deeds
of Bishops of the Hamburg Church* written between 1073 and 1076. He's a Christian,
keen to show the Vikings in a bad light. This is how he described the scene:

*In this temple, entirely decked out in gold, the people worship the statues of three gods
in such wise that the mightiest of them, Thor, occupies a throne in the middle of the
chamber; Wotan and Frikko have places on either side . . . Thor, they say, presides over
the air, which governs the thunder and lightning, the winds and rains, fair weather
and crops. The other, Wotan—that is, the Furious—carries on war and imparts to man
strength against his enemies. The third is Frikko, who bestows peace and pleasure on
mortals. His likeness, too, they fashion with an immense phallus. But Wotan they chisel
armed, as our people are wont to represent Mars. Thor with his scepter apparently
resembles Jove.*

TOM CONROY (PRODUCTION DESIGNER): The real Uppsala (in modern Sweden) is flat as a pancake and not very cinematic. We chose a steep, hilly location in a forest to build our stepped sets, where the actors had a real physical and exhausting engagement with the lie of the land. We based the temple on early Scandinavian stave churches (surviving medieval Scandinavian wooden structures), constructing the first story on location, with higher levels added in VFX. The interiors were built in the studio, the ceiling having been extended by our friends in the VFX department.

KEN GIROTTI (DIRECTOR): We weren't shooting the show in Sweden or anywhere near Uppsala itself—the topography was different, and the temple we could credibly construct could only be a scant representation of what the actual temple was. So, we decided to make a temple—really, a

cathedral—in the forest. Since we were at the "Vatican" of Norse paganism, we wanted to offer the audience something completely unique but also relatable. I asked for a new side of the Vikings to be created, one that was about beauty, ritual, and heightened sexuality. Michael Hirst's script suggested that it should feel like the Viking version of Woodstock, and that's what we tried to do.

JIL TURNER (SET DECORATOR): The sacrificial altar was a key prop for the story. This was originally a table produced by the Naga people of northeastern India that had all the right ingredients, including a beautiful patina, but unfortunately it was very low. I adapted it, realizing that beautiful trees serving as legs were the only solution. The tabletop was then customized with four dug-out grooves configured in a diamond shape that would let the blood merge and drain to a central point.

ABOVE: Early concept art for the Temple at Uppsala, based on an 11th century description by Adam of Bremen.
OPPOSITE: Concept art for the temple interior.

GODS ON THE BATTLEFIELD

SEASON 1, EPISODE 1: "RITES OF PASSAGE"

The opening scene of *Vikings* was intended to set the stage for the series by introducing the themes and main characters, and also by showing how in this series the supernatural world—the world the Vikings believed in—would be tangible, if fleeting. We wanted to see both the physical landscape and also the psychological one. When we, the audience, can—like Ragnar—see (or think we see) Odin on the battlefield, we come to understand not just what the Vikings did but also what they believed.

For any warrior, death in battle was the ideal: It offered the chance to go to Valhalla, "the Hall of the Fallen," in Asgard. Valhalla, with its 540 doors that allowed eight hundred men to leave at once, and its roof of golden shields, was where the Valkyries brought Odin the souls of those who died bravely in battle. Here Odin fed the fallen warriors and gave them mead, so that they would fight for him at Ragnarök, the battle at the end of the world.

But not all fallen warriors went to Valhalla. Half were taken by another group of gods, the Vanir. Those warriors went to Fólkvangr, the "Field of the Host," ruled by the goddess of love and beauty, Freyja, who had her own hall there called Sessrúmnir. It is not known why there were two halls for warriors who fell in battle; some think Fólkvangr may also be where women who died a noble death would find an honorable place to await Ragnarök.

Those who died natural death, not in battle, could not expect such luxury. They were taken to another of the Nine Worlds, Hel, ruled over by a giantess of the same name. Sources differ on who exactly went to Hel and what happened there, but it seems to have been a place where those who had done evil in life were punished. In Hel lay Náströnd, the "Corpse Shore," where the bodies of those guilty of adultery, murder, and oath breaking were punished. Despite its beautiful halls, no warrior would want to end up in Hel; one saga tells of a dying warrior who tried to fool the gods by cutting himself with spears to make it appear he had died in battle.

Creating a sense of this other "world beyond the world" was part of the brief for director of photography P.J. Dillon.

P.J. DILLON (DIRECTOR OF PHOTOGRAPHY): We have used many techniques to create a mystical feel in the show. For instance, on the battlefield in the opening sequence of Season 1, we think we see Odin but aren't quite sure. Are the Valkyries real or simply illusions? We shoot scenes like this with specially shaped anamorphic lenses, as these have a different visual quality to the spherical lenses used in shooting the majority of the show. We also use a lot of filtration in front of the lenses to create distinct and unusual visual characteristics in some scenes (what would have been considered "mistakes" when I began my professional life as a camera trainee!). We embrace and encourage lens flares. We use "lens babies," slant-focus lenses, split-diopters, and other optical techniques depending on the specific requirements of the scene and the director's personal vision of it. We encourage "happy accidents" as a means of creating unique and unusual visual quirks that will set the images apart from the rest of the show—and indeed other shows.

OPPOSITE: Odin's companion. The raven was a magical bird in the eyes of the Vikings, always there to pick over the battlefield remains.

THE STORY OF
THE SEER

The Seer is a figure straight out of the sagas. Odin himself visits a seer to discover the identity of the man who killed his beloved son Baldur. The seer complains that he has to climb out of the wet earth again to answer Odin's questions; in other words, the seer is someone who hovers between life and death, who is hundreds of years old, and who has seen everything in the past and in the future.

—MICHAEL HIRST

Seers—both men and women—are frequently mentioned in sagas and were believed to be able to see the future and read the fate of a man just by looking at him. Seers who were Finns, in particular, were sought out and "paying a visit to the Finns" seems to have been a euphemism for visiting a fortune-teller.

Female Finnish seers often occur in the sagas as the instigators of great quests. One early Icelandic settler was said to have sent three seers on spirit journeys (probably drug-induced trances) to reconnoiter the territory before he set sail.

The Vikings had two words for divination:

Fret—an interrogation or investigation, in which an oracle was asked about the future and the will of the gods. For example, when the Icelandic chieftain Thorkel the Tall asked the god Frey for vengeance upon his enemy Viga-Glum, he asked for a signal that the god had heard him. When the ox he was leading out to sacrifice dropped dead before him, he took this as a sign that Frey had heard him.

Spá—prophecy or divination; it involved casting lots to foretell the future, often using sacred leaves or chips of wood (*blótspánn*). How this was done is uncertain. The Roman historian and senator Tacitus says that during the Roman empire Germanic peoples took a bough cut from a fruit tree and divided into small slips or chips (*surculos*), which were marked with signs (possibly in sacrificial blood) and cast onto a white cloth. How they fell, or which the priest randomly picked up, would then indicate the future.

KARI SKOGLAND (DIRECTOR): We created an otherworldly flavor for the character of the Seer by presenting the scene through slivers and holes in walls to support the disjointed quality of his setting and character. He experiences the world as a blind man, so I thought it would be interesting if we mimicked that feeling. Also, I introduced a snake, a symbol the Seer was afraid of and suggesting a deeper meaning—the underworld—giving the actors something awkward to deal with during the scene.

TOM MCINERNEY (CHIEF MAKEUP ARTIST): Johan Renck, a Season 1 director, wanted the Seer to be unlike anything you might expect someone like to the Seer to look like. We did a series of designs grounding the notion of a mystic and a pagan in reality and came up with what you see on the show today. He's not supposed to have any eyes, but sees in other ways.

OPPOSITE: John Kavanagh as the Seer.

THE SACRIFICES
Season 1, Episode 8: "Sacrifice"

Ragnar comes to Uppsala to attend one of the great Viking religious festivals. Fortunately we have a description of this in Adam of Bremen's chronicle, which provided inspiration for the festival we created:

At nine-year intervals, [there is] a general feast of all the provinces of Sweden . . . The sacrifice is of this nature: Of every living thing that is male, they offer nine heads, with the blood of which it is customary to placate gods of this sort. The bodies they hang in the sacred grove that adjoins the temple. This grove is so sacred in the eyes of the heathen, that each and every tree in it is believed to be divine because of the death or putrefaction of the victims. Even dogs and horses hang there with men.

Sacrifice in Viking culture could take many forms, from the offering of inanimate objects to the death of humans. As we show in the *Vikings* series, the human sacrifices were not necessarily prisoners or slaves; indeed, it could be considered an honor to so die. According to Snorri Sturluson's book *Heimskringla*, the Swedish kings Domalde and Olof Trätälja were both supposedly sacrificed to appease the gods after years of famine. In another *Heimskringla* tale, the Swedish king Aun was said to have sacrificed his nine sons to preserve his own life (nine, as we know, being a magical number for Vikings). After he'd sacrificed the eighth son, however, his people stopped him.

We used some of this historical and mythological detail for *Vikings*, in the Uppsala sequence in Season 1, Episode 8, "Sacrifice." It was the basis for a tense scene in which Athelstan learns he is to be sacrificed but eventually proves unworthy of the Norse gods. The scene showed the Vikings as comfortable with their own culture— and provided a way to view that culture from their perspective, not that of the medieval Christian chroniclers.

KEN GIROTTI (DIRECTOR): I made the priests decidedly effeminate, very un-Viking; that was a conscious choice. Though strangely scarred and decorated, they were intentionally androgynous. Then, when it came to the actual human sacrifice, I wanted the atmosphere to be airy and transcendent, instead of being brooding and dark. The singer we used in the scene of sacrifice was someone I cast expressly for this purpose. I asked her to lift us up: I wanted something otherworldly and yet relatable and beautiful. She certainly delivered.

DONAL LOGUE (KING HORIK): The end of Season 1, in which I sacrifice Leif in the festival, was incredibly moving. It was an honor to be sacrificed; it was an honor to be the one taking life. Where we shot the scene was beautiful, in Wicklow, and a brilliant singer was chanting. The whole experience was a bit magical.

OPPOSITE TOP: Young Björn and Gyda witness the sacrifices at Uppsala with their father.
OPPOSITE BOTTOM: Leif prepares to meet the gods as a human sacrifice.

VIKING NUMEROLOGY

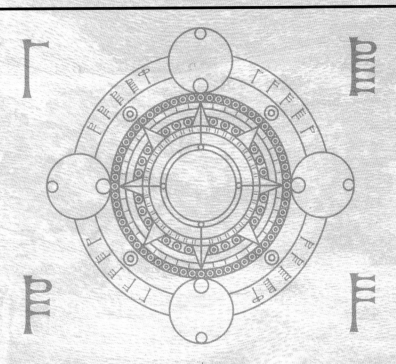

The Vikings believed that some numbers had magical properties, and that anything occurring in these numbers or multiples of them could be a sign from the gods.

The most significant numbers to the Vikings were three and multiples of three. In Viking mythology, there are three races of giants—the frost, fire, and mountain giants; there were three statues in the Temple at Uppsala; the World Tree Yggdrasil has three roots; and only three of Odin's sons survive Ragnarök (Vidar, Baldur, and Hǫðr).

The number nine, being three times three, also was seen to have magical powers. Every ninth year, people from all over Sweden assembled at the Temple at Uppsala to feast for nine days. Nine men were sacrificed during the festival along with nine of each type of animal.

In Viking mythology, Freyr waited nine nights to consummate his union with Gerd; during the last battle, Ragnarök, Thor kills Jörmungandr but staggers back nine steps before falling dead himself. Odin's magical ring Draupnir, forged by the dwarf brothers Eitri and Brokkr, dripped eight golden drops every ninth night to make nine rings of equal weight and worth. There are nine daughters of Aegir, nine mothers of Heimdall, and the giant Thrivaldi has nine heads. And the list goes on.

No one is exactly sure why three and nine are so significant, but it may be related to the old Germanic calendar, which may have been based on lunar months. The time it takes the moon to return to a given position among the stars is just a little over twenty-seven days, which is divisible by nine and three. The only medieval source to mention this system is the early English Christian writer the Venerable Bede, who records the old Germanic Anglo-Saxon calendar in his book *De temporum ratione* (*On the Reckoning of Time*), written in 725. As the lunar month is shorter than the solar month, Bede records that the Germanic system had an extra "leap month" added in the middle of summer.

OPPOSITE: Nine of everything. Nine of every beast were sacrificed at Uppsala once every nine years.
FOLLOWING SPREAD: The Vikings believed that the World Tree known as Ygdrassil bound together the Nine Worlds of men, gods, and supernatural creatures.

CHAPTER
5
LEGENDS

ASLAUG ON THE NINE WORLDS:

WHEN OUR CHILDREN ARE YOUNG, they look out across the sea and ask us, "What lies beyond the horizon?" And we smile and gather them in by the fire. We tell them:

In the beginning there were two worlds, Niflheim, where all was dark and ice, and Muspellsheim, which brimmed with fire and light. Between the two was a great emptiness where the frost and fire met, and where the frost giant Ymir appeared. Here too the gods emerged, including the greatest of these, Odin. It was Odin who made the world of men, Midgard, with his brothers when they killed the giant. Now the earth is his flesh, the rocks his shattered teeth, his blood has become the rivers and lakes, and his skull is the sky. It was Odin who then first put men on this world. Then he drew night and day apart and sent them circling through the skies with the girl, Sun, and the boy, Moon, who run forever, chased by wolves.

Then the gods, whom we call the Aesir, built a home of their own—Asgard. And each day they cross from Asgard over the burning rainbow bridge, Bifröst, to the holy well where they hold their court.

Beyond the palaces of Asgard, across the river Ifing, lies Jötunheimr, the realm of the giants, who will bring the end of the world, which we call "Ragnarök." Its ruler is King Thrym, who once stole Thor's hammer.

But there are other worlds. Vanaheim is the land of the other gods, the Vanir, who fought the Aesir long ago, from where the god Freyr first came as a hostage to Asgard. The Vanir can see the future and bring wisdom and fertility in their path.

Svartálfaheimr is the place of the dwarfs who work in the mountains and make the magical things that the gods and men covet. Álfheimr is the realm of the light elves, who are fairer to look upon than the sun.

And then there is the ninth world, which we call Hel. Here the unglorious dead, denied the company of Odin in Valhalla, wait for the end of time.

These are the Nine Worlds bound together by the great ash tree whose name is Yggdrasil. It has three great roots, which reach to the realms of the gods and the giants, and into Hel. Beneath the giants' root lies Mimir's well, which brought wisdom and understanding to Odin and all those who drank of it. Beneath the gods' root lies the well that we call Urðr. Here the Norns, who rule the fate of both men and gods, take water and white clay and shower it on Yggdrasil so it will never rot away. The water falls back to earth as dew. It is the Norns who, at your birth, wove the web of fate that you can never escape.

The tree is not a quiet place. At the base of the third root lies the creature Niðhǫggr, gnawing at the tree, and atop its highest branch sits an eagle, whose wing beats bring the breath of wind to the world of men. The squirrel Ratatoskr runs between the two, carrying insults from one to the other. Amid the high branches, four harts chew at the tree's new shoots. But Yggdrasil lives on, forever green.

This is what lies high above in the wide-blue heaven, and deep below in the caves of the earth, and in the beginning and the end.

This is what lies beyond the horizon.

THE STORY OF
JARL BORG

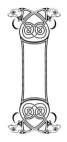

Jarl Borg, or Earl Borg, is an enemy of King Horik's who becomes—when the two ally— also an enemy of Ragnar's. Shrewd, ambitious, and quintessentially Viking in outlook and behavior, Borg invades Ragnar's territory and tries to destroy his family. For Ragnar there is no greater crime. However long it takes, he will have his revenge, and his revenge will be spectacular.

—MICHAEL HIRST

Jarl Borg represents one of the many powerful warlords in early ninth-century Scandinavia whose exploits were slowly forging disparate tribes into nations. Coming from Götaland, one of the three traditional parts of Sweden (known as "lands"), Borg is of the people known as Geats—a group celebrated in one of the great epic poems of the era, *Beowulf*—whose king Hrothgar, lived in the gilded hall Heorot.

Jarl Borg does not have the wealth or reach of *Beowulf*'s Hrothgar, and, for *Vikings*, Michael Hirst wove him a deep backstory, showing how the fickleness of fate as much as the intentions of men could make or break a Viking's career. Jarl Borg is closely involved in the struggles for land and power that typified the lives of real earls at this time. He is a man with a tragic past who faces what he sees as repeated betrayals by Ragnar and King Horik. Borg is a man keenly aware that, with support and land, he might be as much of a king as Horik or indeed the ever-ambitious Ragnar. But this is not what the fates have in store for Borg. His is an ambition that will end in horror.

THORBJØRN HARR (JARL BORG): Michael Hirst had written such a fantastic backstory for my character that I had a lot to build the character around. I built my portrayal of Jarl Borg around the loss of his loved ones, and the betrayal by his own brother. So, of course, when Jarl Borg is betrayed again, he strikes back with a fury that comes from somewhere deep down in his soul. The way we played out the story, although it ended in a brutal way, there was some kind of mutual respect between Ragnar and Jarl Borg. In a different situation, I believe, they could easily have raided alongside each other.

In my mind, Jarl Borg really had a deep love for his first wife. The genius little detail—to carry her skull around—is something I loved to play around with. The observant viewer will notice that I have her skull with me even from the first episode in Season 2. But it's not revealed until later that it's the skull of my first wife. In the scene where I'm addressing her skull, I thought it would be fun to turn it around and drink from it at the end. It took some effort from the prop department to make the skull into a solid beer mug.

KEN GIROTTI (DIRECTOR): Jarl Borg's attack on Kattegat while Ragnar is away in Wessex was a kind of logistical precursor for me to a very large assault from water that the Vikings make early in Season 3. Both battles combine work from the water leading to taking beachheads and attacking up onto land . . . a bit of D-Day on *Vikings*! Very difficult, but very much fun to plan and shoot.

OPPOSITE: Thorbjørn Harr as Jarl Borg.

THE STORY OF
ASLAUG

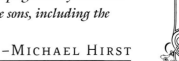

Aslaug is a princess whose father was the famous warrior Sigurd, the central character in the Völsungasaga, *who slew the dragon Fafnir. She appears unexpectedly in Ragnar's life just as his marriage is under strain, and becomes pregnant by him. She replaces Lagertha as Ragnar's wife and bears him several more sons, including the infamous and brutal Ivar the Boneless.*

—MICHAEL HIRST

According to the *Saga of Ragnar Lodbrok*, Aslaug was the daughter of the shield maiden Brynhildr. She was discovered by Ragnar while bathing and he instantly fell in love with her. She bore him all his most famous children, including Björn Ironside, Hvitserk, Ragnvald, and Ivar the Boneless.

Aslaug's parents were two of the greatest heroes from Norse mythology. Sigurd is the same character as Siegfried in the German *Nibelungenlied*, the source for composer Richard Wagner's Ring cycle of operas. In the *Völsungasaga*, Sigurd is asked by his foster father to kill Fafnir, the son of the dwarf king, who has taken a great treasure given to him by the gods in compensation for their killing of his brother Ótr. In this treasure is a cursed ring that turns Fafnir into a dragon. Sigurd has the magical sword Gram forged, then digs a pit and waits for Fafnir to walk over it. When he does, Sigurd stabs Fafnir with the sword, killing him. He then bathes in the dragon's blood, which grants him invulnerability, and drinks some as well, which allows him to understand the language of birds. The birds tell him his foster father has also been tainted by the ring, so Sigurd kills him before eating the dragon's heart—which grants him the gift of prophecy.

It is after this that Sigurd meets Brynhildr, who promises herself to him but prophesies that he will marry someone else. At some point here the two also conceive Aslaug, although the *Völsungasaga* is unclear about when. Sigurd goes to live at the court of King Gjúki, whose wife, Grimhild, covets the ring and the treasure. She brews an "ale of forgetfulness" that makes Sigurd forget Brynhildr, and he marries the queen's daughter. The queen then tries to marry her son Gudrun to Brynhildr, but Gudrun cannot reach her castle, which is protected by a ring of fire. Sigurd agrees to change places with Gudrun, crosses the fire, and wins her hand on Gudrun's behalf. Brynhildr discovers the truth and arranges for Sigurd to be murdered in his sleep. She then throws herself onto his funeral pyre so she can join him in Hel.

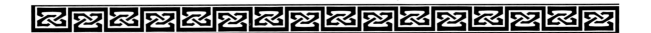

ALYSSA SUTHERLAND (ASLAUG): Aslaug never had to struggle with having food put on the table, but I think she's struggled emotionally and had very traumatic things happen to her early on, with the death of her parents and growing up an orphan, that affect the way she interacts with people.

I love that, throughout the series, the Viking women like Aslaug are shown next to women from the same time period in England and, in Season 3, France. It's a wonderful juxtaposition. You see the Viking women leading their towns, fighting alongside the men, demanding divorces. They truly have their own voice, which was a surprise to me and a delight to play with as an actress.

For all of Season 2, I think I was so consumed with performing well I didn't sit back and enjoy the moment as much as I could have! I've relaxed a bit now and there are some real standout moments in Season 3 that I loved for Aslaug. When she finally finds her voice with Ragnar, and tells him that she doesn't like him leaving his sons behind time and time again,

that was really special. And the scene in Episode 10 of Season 3 ["The Dead"] when she runs the *ping*, was great. The extras were really loud and boisterous, and it was so much fun (for me and for Aslaug).

KATHERYN WINNICK (LAGERTHA): I tried to make creative choices with Lagertha's relationships with both Siggy and Aslaug that were against stereotype. Most of the fans expected animosity between our characters, but I chose to take the other route. I feel that Lagertha understands and sympathizes with Aslaug. She knows it's not easy to be married to Ragnar Lothbrok and to be, in effect, a single mother whenever he is off raiding and pillaging.

TRAVIS FIMMEL (RAGNAR LOTHBROK): My favorite scenes in the whole series would be the scenes with my two wives in the first episodes of Season 2. Purely because they left some of the humor in them.

ABOVE: Sailing out of legend. Aslaug (Alyssa Sutherland) approaches Kattegat.

DRESSING ASLAUG

Aslaug represents one of the truly powerful women we know existed in Viking society during a time when the role of women in Christian European states was often very restricted. She also represents a character whose biography is a combination of history and mythology, something very usual at the time. It was quite common for a king to claim descent from Odin or a great mythological hero of the past; such semi-legendary family trees helped to give the stories of the age some personal truth. Those listening to tales of heroes and dragons could claim descent from the characters they were hearing about. Aslaug claimed perhaps the two greatest Germanic heroes as her parents; she was the daughter of a dragon slayer and a shield maiden, and a shield maiden in her own right. In this she represents not just a powerful Viking, she demonstrates how the Vikings liked to see themselves.

JOAN BERGIN (COSTUME DESIGNER): It was such a treat when I was handed a rich princess-daughter-of-Brunhilde-of-Wagner fame. Add to this the actress is six feet tall and a natural clotheshorse. Her arrival into Kattegat with six hand-maidens and an eight-month, magnificent pregnancy bump, and swathed head to toe in silken wools and royal purple furs, was one of the visual highlights of Season 2. Since she bore Ragnar four sons in quick succession, we ran an exquisite line in royal maternity wear. All we had learned and practiced in the workshop about Viking craft, we were able to exalt further because of Aslaug's higher royal lineage and wealth.

ALYSSA SUTHERLAND (ASLAUG): Joan creates clothing that make you feel so part of the time period. Aslaug cares very much about where she came from, and now her status in Kattegat, and Joan's costumes for her definitely reflect that pride.

DEE CORCORAN (CHIEF HAIR DESIGNER): Aslaug is very much a princess. Unlike the shield maidens, her look is much more feminine and fluid, in response to her soft nature.

ABOVE: Daughter of the dragon slayer. Aslaug is a princess born of mythological parents.
OPPOSITE: Alyssa Sutherland as Aslaug.

THE SONS OF RAGNAR

The sons of Ragnar are some of the most important characters in Norse mythology and history. Stories about them figure in contemporary chronicles, and elaborate tales about them were told in the more fictional sagas, including the *Tale of the Sons of Ragnar*. So impressive indeed were the stories told that many a Viking leader who was no relation at all would later claim to be a "son of Ragnar."

BJÖRN IRONSIDE

Björn, one of the semi-legendary kings of early Sweden, conducted many Viking raids with his brother (the possibly adopted) Hastein. The most daring of these was a plan to sack Rome itself—which formed the inspiration for the denouement of Episode 10 in Season 3, where Ragnar tricks his way into Paris. While Hastein continued raiding after his Mediterranean expedition, Björn went home and retired, living out his life as a rich man.

HASTEIN

Hastein was considered to be one of the greatest Viking warlords of all time. He is first recorded taking part in the Viking attack on Noirmoutier in AD 843 and was on the Loire again in 859 before his great raid into the Mediterranean. On returning home, Hastein put together the last Viking force to invade England in Alfred the Great's reign. However, after a lifetime of Viking attacks, the Anglo-Saxons of Wessex were now well prepared for this raid, and Hastein's forces were eventually routed. Hastein disappears from the historical record in the year 896.

IVAR THE BONELESS

According to the sagas, Aslaug prophesied to Ragnar on their wedding night that if they slept together over the next three days, their first child would be born deformed. Ragnar laughed and took her by force, and the result was Ivar the Boneless.

Just what was meant by "boneless" is still uncertain. Some scholars have suggested that he may have suffered from a serious genetic disorder, perhaps the brittle-bone disease osteogenesis imperfecta, which left him unable to walk. The Old Norse *inn beinlausi*—meaning "boneless" or "legless"—might have been a misreading (or mis-hearing) of *inn barnlausi*—"the childless one"; or, perhaps, even the Latin *exosus*—"hateful"—was misheard as exos—meaning "boneless."

Certainly Ivar had gained a reputation that would have made him hateful in the eyes of those he crossed, Christian and Viking alike. And, as for being childless, the *Tale of the Sons of Ragnar* says Ivar was childless not due to any genetic problem but "because of the way he was, with no lust or love, but not short on cunning or cruelty."

In AD 866, Ivar and his brothers Ubbe and Halfdan crossed the North Sea to England to be revenged on those who had killed Ragnar. In the next twenty years, they would destroy many of the old kingdoms of England, Ireland, and Scotland. Ivar disappears from the historic record sometime after the year 870. His ultimate fate is uncertain but his death is recorded in the *Annals of Ulster*.

SIGURD SNAKE-IN-THE-EYE

Sigurd was born with a deviated pupil, as his mother Aslaug had prophesied, and which she claimed proved that her own father was the legendary Sigurd, slayer of the dragon Fafnir. According to the *Tale of the Sons of Ragnar*, Sigurd inherited Zealand, Scania, and Halland from his father and married the daughter of King Aelle of Northumbria, the man who had murdered his father, and who would later himself be executed in the blood-eagle ceremony by Sigurd's brother Ivar. Sigurd's grandson was Gorm the Old, the first historically recognized king of Denmark.

HALFDAN

Halfdan went to raid England with Ivar and led the army against the grandson of King Ecbert of Wessex, Alfred the Great, at Ashdown—a battle that Alfred won. Halfdan later ruled London before moving to York. He was allegedly expelled from the city for his cruelty and died on another Viking expedition. The sources for this period are meager and confusing; he may be the same person as another "son of Ragnar"—Hvitserk. According to the sagas, Hvitserk helped his brothers avenge his father's death and then went raiding among the Viking Rus (the Vikings of Russia, Belarus, and Ukraine). Overwhelmed by the enemy, Hvitserk was captured and asked how he wished to die. He opted to be burned alive.

UBBE

Ubbe attacked England with the historically attested Great Heathen Army, which Saxon chroniclers recorded attacking the Wessex of Alfred the Great. Ubbe took a fleet around the English coast to launch a diversionary attack on the West Country near Combwich in AD 878 but was spectacularly and surprisingly defeated by the Earl of Devon, a defeat put down to the failure of Ubbe's magical silk raven banner. A real example of one of these, possibly even this one, survives and is now in Scotland, where it is known as the "fairy flag of Dunvegan." Ubbe died in the battle.

ABOVE: Ragnar with Aslaug and their son Hvitserk (Cathal O'Hallin).

CHAPTER
6

THE LAW

LAGERTHA ON WOMEN AND THE LAW:

I HAVE HEARD IT SAID THAT, among the Franks, the women belong to their men, as toys belong to children. It is not that way with us. In the north, where the winters are dark and hard, there is a deal to be struck between men and women. It begins at the gathering where fathers and brothers find us husbands and make the pact to join two families together. A good father asks his daughter her opinion, for a bad match may end in death. But it is his match to make. Love may follow one day. Few men or women would dare to love first.

It is the husband's place to travel and trade and hunt—that is his role—but it is for the wife to rule the home. Step over the threshold and you enter her world. True, it is a world of cooking and weaving and tending the children and farm, but a Norse woman is no possession. On her belt you will see the keys to every lock in the house; the treasure, the land, and all the family has is in her care. The possessions are hers.

A wife must be strong—strong to rule the home when husbands tarry abroad, sometimes for years. Strong to chide her man when he flees from insults and set him instead on a course of bloody revenge. Strong, too, to throw her cloak over his drawn sword when he rushes foolishly into the fray and so prevent a disaster. And brave indeed is the man who will not be so ruled. Many a wife has repaid a slap from her husband with the point of a dagger, and none have blamed her. To strike a woman is a deadly insult.

Now the women of the Franks are stuck with boorish husbands, for a possession cannot leave its owner. If our men fail us in battle, or in providing for our family, or prove weak and impotent, then our bond is broken. The wife will take her witnesses first to the door and then to the bedside and declare there that the marriage is over. The husband must then return her dowry and other gifts and leave. With just these few words, she is then free. And if her husband's doom is to die, she may choose from all other men or live without, as she wishes. She is the mistress of her own fate and deals in the world on her own terms.

And what of the shield maidens that the skalds sing of? It is not for every girl to become another Brynhildr. We may rule the home but not the whole world, and fathers would deem it a sin for their daughters to wear the clothes of men. The wife gains her will through the words she whispers to her husband, and through her magic.

There are those of us for whom honor is the real master. To become a shield maiden is to bear a burning wrong that can only be put right in battle. To fight for oneself when it is one's own pride at stake and when men alone cannot bear the weight. At Brávellir, where Sigurd Ring and Harald Wartooth fought, where the heroes Ubbe and Are the One-Eyed, Grette the Evil, and Einar the Fatbellied clashed, it was the three hundred shield maidens who held the field. Though small of frame, a shield maiden is the match for any man, avenging past insults not with words but with iron. She is respected by her fellow warriors and feared by her enemies.

No other race has women like these.

THE STORY OF
KING HORIK

King Horik enters Ragnar's life during the nine-yearly pagan festival at Uppsala, where nine of everything, including humans, are sacrificed to the gods. Early ninth-century Scandinavia is divided not into countries but into many small and competing kingdoms, and Horik rules one of these. A charming, immensely sympathetic character, he appears to want to hitch his star to Ragnar's, but, in truth, he has no intention of allowing Ragnar to become more famous or successful than himself.

*—*MICHAEL HIRST

Horik Gudfredsson was a ruler over the Danes in the early Viking age, defending his people against the Christian Franks then ruled by Charlemagne's son, Louis the Pious. When Christian missionaries began appearing in his lands, Horik, furiously proud of his pagan heritage, responded by invading Germany and destroying Hamburg Cathedral.

This raid helped usher in the era of Viking raids in Europe, although Horik himself later disowned them, fearful that the Viking warlords he had helped to create, now rich with plunder, might one day turn on him. Despite all his protestations of innocence to the courts of Europe, Horik was probably taking a cut of the plunder from the war bands. He was right to fear his own warlords, however, as he would eventually be killed by one of them.

DONAL LOGUE (KING HORIK): Fortunately for me, Horik was one of the first really known Viking kings (there's even a statue of him in Denmark). Horik, it seemed, had tremendous power as a king and had to overcome many hurdles to gain the throne. To get to the top of the heap in the Viking world was never the mere result of birth—it had to be earned. That being said, I think his greatest skill was of a deceptive nature—to triangulate people and pit rivals and enemies against each other, and to temper the flight of those close to him by clipping their wings a bit. When he meets Ragnar and accepts his fealty, Horik very deliberately (and seemingly casually) throws him headfirst against his biggest rival, Jarl Borg. It proves to be cataclysmic for all involved. So is Horik a deceiver or a survivor? Most likely he managed to survive and thrive for so long because mastering deception was a big part of his game.

What I liked most about Horik was his sense of humor and the playful side to his deviousness. I loved being introduced as someone who disguised himself as a peasant and kicked the priests in the temple, knowing full well they might (or might not) feel the measure of his wrath once his true identity was revealed. He had a kind of power that allows for a lot of arbitrary behavior. I don't think he abused that the way someone like Henry VIII or Stalin did, to give some examples. But ultimately the political and social paradigm in which *Vikings* is set didn't have room for both Horik and Ragnar, and Horik had to go.

OPPOSITE: Donal Logue as King Horik Gudfredsson.
PREVIOUS SPREAD: Lagertha and Aslaug ruling the home.

THE STORY OF
PORUNN

Porunn is an ex-slave, a beautiful young woman who attracts Björn's attentions—but is initially too frightened to respond to them. Björn manages to persuade her that his interest is genuine, and Aslaug, seeing the growing attachment, makes Porunn a free woman. But Porunn's problem is that she wants to be more Viking than the Vikings. She wants to fight in the battle lines, despite being pregnant. And the consequences of her actions will be devastating.

—MICHAEL HIRST

Slaves like Porunn were a valuable trade item in the Viking age. Although mythology suggested that these *prælls* ("thralls") as they were known, were descended from a race born to serve, many people could become slaves. Ordinary people captured in raids, like Athelstan, could be sold into slavery, providing a useful additional income for the raiders. High-status captives might be ransomed with the threat of selling them as slaves as well if their families didn't pay up. Even among the peoples of Scandinavia, it was not unusual for Norwegians to keep Swedish *prælls* or Danes to keep Finns.

Male *prælls* in the Viking age usually provided unskilled labor, performing the most menial and physically toughest roles—from building walls and digging peat to herding animals. Female *prælls* worked around the farm, grinding flour, milking, washing, and acting as personal maids or even bed slaves.

The signs of the *præll* were the slave collar around the neck and short-cropped hair. The usual costume was a simple tunic or shift of undyed homespun cloth.

The child of a slave was always a slave, no matter the rank of his father. *Wergild* (blood money) was not paid for slaves, although a man who killed another man's slave owed him damages, just as if he had killed his cow or pig. Slaves were not entirely without rights, however. A slave owner had to provide medical care and a living for *prælls* who were injured or crippled in their service. Most slaves could not own property and could not be married. The exception to this was in cases where the slave owner allowed the *præll* to work a small portion of land, the proceeds of which were owned by the slave. *Prælls* could also sell any cottage crafts they produced in their free time. The *præll's* goal in life was simple—to accumulate enough money to eventually purchase his or her own freedom.

GAIA WEISS (PORUNN): Porunn was raised as a slave. She has only known serfdom and brutality, and suffered enormously both physically and emotionally. She says to Björn, one of the first times they speak to each other: "People like me don't have hopes or dreams."

We initially shot a scene for Season 2 where Lagertha went to Porunn and told her: "I was once like you." To me, that's when things fell into place for Porunn. Hearing from someone she admires that things can change gives her hope for the first time.

This is what motivates her to train as a shield maiden.

Everyone, at some point in life, has been frustrated in a situation where another person (a teacher, administration, customs official, etc.) was able to exercise power over them. You're powerless in the face of injustice, and any attempt to justify yourself would make things worse. That was a very useful feeling to play Porunn as a slave.

I loved following Porunn as she became a woman and then a mother. I think my favorite scene we shot so far is when she gave birth. It was emotionally draining. It was the first time I couldn't relate to my character's experience, but the challenge made it more exciting.

ABOVE: Gaia Weiss as Porunn.
OPPOSITE: Porrun, the slave who would be more Viking than her masters.

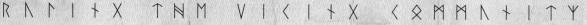

RULING THE VIKING COMMUNITY

The government of Viking society was in the hands of assemblies of freemen. In these councils, known as *þings* ("things"), disputes were solved and political decisions were made. The assemblies were open to all the freemen of a country, province or area—but not women or slaves or children. There was a hierarchy of *þings*: A local assembly might send a decision up to an area *þing*, which might in turn send representatives to a national *þing*.

The locations for *þings*—central and easily accessible—and the fact that they met at regular intervals also made them ideas for trading and religious ceremonies so the assembly was not necessarily just a dry meeting but could be a festival and a market. It was also where marriages were decided. The *þing* was typically held at the same specially designated place, often a field or common, like Þingvellir, the old location of the Icelandic thing (Alþingi). The parliament of the Isle of Man,

which was a Viking stronghold, is still named after the meeting place of the *þing*, Tynwald— which means the same as *þingvellir* (the field of the "*þing*").

At the *þing*, the "law speaker" would recite the law, which he had memorized. His job was not to tell the people what to do—as an Anglo-Saxon king might—but to rehearse the law, make judgments based on the extant laws, and also to formally codify any new laws that the people might decide upon. He was the repository of local custom and stories to be consulted during discussions; he presided over a relatively democratic process, something very unusual at this time. Each case was voted on by the members of the *þing*, with each man getting one vote. The decisions included the election of chieftains and kings. In fact, of course, powerful clans and individuals could dominate, ensuring policy went their way, as we see happening with King Horik.

THE BLOOD EAGLE

SEASON 2, EPISODE 7: "BLOOD EAGLE"

The blood eagle was a punishment we know of from a number of Viking sources. The early-eleventh-century skaldic poet Sigvatr is the first to mention it. He wrote, in a poem of praise for the later English king Cnut, "Ivar, who dwelt in York, carved the eagle on Aelle's back."

This is a reference to Ragnar's son Ivar the Boneless, who revenged himself on Aelle, king of Northumbria. According to the legend, Aelle later lost a battle to Ivar; captured, Aelle was brought before Ragnar's son as he reveled in his victory. Seeing the humbled Northumbrian king before him, Ivar ordered him sacrificed to Odin, in thanks for the victory, in the ceremony of the blood eagle. By the time the thirteenth-century *Tale of the Sons of Ragnar* was written, the scene is further described; it involved hacking open the victim's chest and removing his lungs so they resembled the folded wings of a bloody eagle.

The Vikings thought of the eagle as a carrion bird that eats the flesh of dead animals and the dead of battle. They knew it as *hræsvelgr*, which translates as "corpse-guzzler." The eagle was also associated with Odin, as are those other carrion birds, ravens, although this connection may go back further, perhaps even to the days of the Roman empire. The imperial eagle was the symbol of Roman might, and the Germanic tribes along the Roman frontier may have taken on this idea and associated the bird with their own overlord, Odin.

THORBJØRN HARR (JARL BORG): The blood-eagle scene is one of the most demanding things I have ever done as an actor. It was physically very exhausting, and quite painful too. But on a personal level it was also very special. We shot that scene on my very last day on the set of *Vikings*. So it wasn't just a farewell to the character, it also became a farewell to all of my colleagues. The friendship and support among the cast members on *Vikings* is astonishing. Being executed in such a way, in front of absolutely everyone of the cast, became a very personal experience.

KARI SKOGLAND (DIRECTOR): It was far better to suggest than to actually see what was happening—which is too horrific to contemplate—so I focused on how it was affecting the characters. Some couldn't bear to watch, others took pleasure in it, while others tried to muster their own courage. For Ragnar there was a layer of sympathy. He had to do what was necessary yet at some level he wanted Jarl Borg to withstand the pain and succeed—if Borg could do that then he would die an honorable man and Ragnar was part of that

success. Both found an honor in his death. Borg was all about redemption. Once he realized that there was no way out and he was going to die, that all he had left was dignity, it switched the gears to going with grace. As a result, the entire event becomes very emotional.

P.J. DILLON (DIRECTOR OF PHOTOGRAPHY): My favorite scene is probably the "Blood Eagle"—a huge set piece, with seven minutes of screen time, all of the principal cast, and about a hundred extras. Kari and I decided to only use flame, i.e., no artificial lighting at all. This was a huge undertaking for the special effects department but they made it work. The bulk of the scene was also shot on a very rare and specialized lens, a Panavision Super Speed T1 lens. We used this lens "wide open"—which meant that our focus-puller, Alan Butler, had a virtually impossible task. At times there was practically no margin of error, and this was compounded by the fact that the bulk of the scene was shot on Steadicam. That was a challenge.

OPPOSITE: Thorbjørn Harr as Jarl Borg.
FOLLOWING SPREAD: A Viking longship returns to the calm waters of the fjord.

CHAPTER

7

THE SEA

FLOKI ON THE DRAGON SHIPS:

THE WORLD IS FULL OF SHIPS. I have seen the barges of the Rus as they wallow in the waves and the Arab galleys of the southern sea, but there are none like our *drakkars*, the dragon ships, that take us to new lands. Our ships begin in the forest, with their roots still alive in the ground. A shipwright can see the planks still inside the tree and cut only the best. The key is to work with the tree, using its natural curves and branchings to make each piece of the hull.

We start with the strong keel that holds the frames, like a man's ribs. Around the frames we build up planks for the sides, each one overlapping the last, and between each plank we push tarred cow hair to make a seal. A seagoing ship must live with the waves, and so we build our ships not to fight the ocean but to bend to it. I build the hull around a *meginhufr*—a strong middle plank. Below the *meginhufr*, I cleat and lash the planks to the frames without nails, so they can move against each other, letting my ship slide over the waves. It is for this that people call these ships "dragon ships" or "serpent ships"—for they snake over the sea.

Above the *meginhufr*, the ship must be a fortress if the sea is not to overwhelm us. Here the planks are nailed fast and the oars run out through holes below the top plank so the sides may be built up high. Each hole can be shut fast when the nine billow maidens, daughters of the sea god Aegir and his wife Rán, rage against us.

The wind is the sailor's friend but a fickle one. For this reason, our *drakkars* carry both sail and oars. At sea, with a favorable wind, our fine woolen sail is hoisted on sealskin ropes and drives us forward. When the wind fails, or when it is time to slip unnoticed up the rivers of hostile lands, the sail and mast may be stowed away; we row silently through the still night. It is then we take out our richly carved prow figures and place them at the bow that they might see the way and strike terror into those who would stop us.

But for all the shipwright's craft, a steed is only as good as his mount. The sea has no landmarks to guide us, so it is a brave man who takes the steering oar and turns his prow to the horizon beyond sight of land. For the most part, it is best to travel the coast, where mountains and inlets guide the way. Beyond the horizon, you must be guided by the sun and stars and travel with one who has taken the path before and knows where it will lead. I have heard that some take ravens on such adventures and, far beyond land, release them that they might fly up high and see over the horizon to lands beyond the sight of men. The birds will then fly off there, and the happy sailors will follow their course. Pity the crew whose raven returns having seen nothing but billowing waves.

There are other ways I have heard speak of that can take a man across open water. And there are rich lands beyond the horizon that would reward such a hero, but these are secret things and should not be spoken of here.

DESIGNING THE BOATS

The most famous Viking ships from archaeological contexts, and hence the ones most commonly illustrated in books on Viking history, are the Gokstad and Oseberg ships, which were probably trade or pleasure craft. The most famous of these is the beautifully preserved Oseberg ship, which was possibly the pleasure yacht of Queen Åsa Haraldsdottir of Agder, who died right in the middle of our period, ca. AD 834. This was the Viking equivalent of a medieval royal barge. The ship was preserved because it had been placed in a Norwegian burial mound, along with the remains of its owner and an opulent set of grave goods—all of which were excavated in 1904 and 1905.

While the Oseberg ship gives us an idea of the technical skill available in ship-building and the virtuoso decoration that sometimes accompanies this, the main type of ship we use in *Vikings* is quite different, as most of our ships are *drakkars*– warships. We have fewer archaeological examples of these to work with but a couple have been found. The Roskilde longship is an eleventh-century vessel excavated from a fjord where it had been deliberately sunk to block a navigable channel and hence protect the town from a seaborne attack. The Ladby ship was interred in the only known ship grave in Denmark and was buried around AD 925 with its owner.

From these finds and from our meager written and illustrative sources we know that all longships used a single square-rigged sail made of a finely woven, home-spun wool cloth known as *vathmal*, secured with ropes made of seal or walrus skin. *Drakkars* also carried removable prow figures of many different types, and their masts could be "unstepped" for safety, storage, or stealth.

Practical considerations limited what sort of ships we could build for *Vikings*. As the rigging from a Viking vessel has never been discovered, no one knows for sure how these ships were rigged. We rig our replicas with a simple square sail; there are some contemporary drawings of these. More adventurous academics have claimed the sails may have been more like vast stunt kites, like the type used by kite-surfers—effectively, wings.

Actual Viking longships might be 18 feet wide and 80 feet long, but production had to consider what could be safely transported to the various required locations in Ireland on trailers. So we made our boats two to three inches smaller than the maximum legal road dimensions of 56 feet by 12 feet by 12 feet. Even then, a trailer had to be specially constructed that could lift the ships over especially narrow gateways.

TOM CONROY (PRODUCTION DESIGNER): Exploring museums and Viking replica ships in Scandinavia, I soon found out that it was not very practical or affordable to transport extant ships to Ireland. Besides, we would also need two identical ships—one for the water, and another for a gimbal/green-screen arrangement. The chances of finding twin ships of the scale we needed were nil—so, with the help of set designer and art director Jon Beer, we worked out the lines of our ships, drawing on Scandinavian museums and rare shipbuilding books.

We explored traditional boatbuilders throughout Europe and finally found longboat specialist Radim Zapetal, in

OPPOSITE TOP: Just as in battle, lines of shields provided protection for the ship's crew.
OPPOSITE RIGHT: Richly carved figureheads gave Viking warcraft the name "dragonships."
OPPOSITE LEFT: Concept art for the dragon head on Ragnar's ship.

Moravia, in landlocked Czech Republic, of all places. He and his brilliant team worked twelve-hour days for four months and created the two longships, very much using the old Viking techniques, but with the aid of hand power tools. The two ships would be transported by land, all the way across Europe, in a special outsize convoy to Rotterdam, Holland—then by ship to the old Viking port of . . . Dublin.

TRAVIS FIMMEL (RAGNAR LOTHBROK): I could never survive a long sea voyage with a boat full of actors, including myself.

KEN GIROTTI (DIRECTOR): Much of the storm footage is shot on a boat sitting on a hydraulic gimbal, which simulates movement. This is set up in front of a green-screen, computer-generated background storm with added wind and spray. As crazy as that sounds, it's actually more controllable to do that than it is to get the boats out onto the water on a calm day and try to get them all into one shot.

BILL HALLIDAY (VFX PRODUCER): The storm-at-sea sequence in Season 2, Episode 2, was definitely our most challenging sequence to that point. We shot the sequence against a very large green screen that was built specifically for the scene at the back of the studio. Engineers had built a hydraulic gimbal substantial enough to support the weight of the forty-six-foot hero boat and twenty-odd crew.

Ciaran Donnelly, the episode director, had showed us a lot of examples from the show *Deadliest Catch* and explained that that was the level of storm he was after. We actually contacted *Deadliest Catch* and purchased some B-roll footage that we ended up using for some of the backgrounds, but, for the most part, the backgrounds were 100 percent digital. The water was generated through a computer simulation that was the most computationally intensive work we've done on the show. The cliffs were created as a matte painting that was projected on to a 3D-modeled surface to give it dimension.

JEFF WOOLNOUGH (DIRECTOR): The boats are not precision vehicles. They don't have keels, so steering them is a challenge. The best part of the ships is when we're out on the water with all the boats and two hundred mariners and our actors all made up and costumed. It's absolutely magical.

CLIVE STANDEN (ROLLO): When we film the boat sequences for the show, there are definitely days where you realize it must have been miserable being a Viking at sea. Don't get me wrong: When we are at full sail on the Irish Sea and the wind is blowing through your hair and the sun is beating down on the deck, it's beautiful out on the water. But filming on a gimbal with nowhere to shelter from the incessant rain machines beating down? You start to realize how hard it would have been crossing the open ocean with just a sun stone and a sun shadow board, completely at the mercy of the elements.

ABOVE: The sun compass that Ragnar uses to sail to the shores of England.

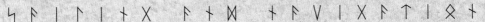

SAILING AND NAVIGATION

Setting up Ragnar as a man willing to set sail into the open, unknown ocean gave us the opportunity to explore some of the theories about how the Vikings managed to cross open sea without modern navigational aids.

Most Viking ships traveled coastal routes so they were always in sight of land. That way, all you needed to know was the coast, its landmarks, and where the shoals and rocks were, to navigate safely. Using fixed visual references like this is usually called "pilotage."

Beyond sight of land, things got harder. Flóki Vilgerðarson, who the *Icelandic Book of Settlements* (*Landnámabók*) credited as being the first person to deliberately set out for Iceland, navigated using ravens. When he reached the Faroe Islands, about two hundred miles from Scotland, he took three ravens on board and headed off in the rough direction of Iceland. After a while he released a raven, which flew up until it could see much farther over the horizon than Flóki could, at which point it spotted the Faroes and promptly flew back home. Some time later, he set another raven free: It flew up, had a look around, and promptly came back to the deck, indicating that they were really now quite a long way from land. Finally he let the third raven go; it flew up, spotted Iceland in the far distance, and headed off there. Flóki gratefully followed.

In the *History of the Faroes*, a Viking instrument called the "sun shadow board," or *Solskuggefjøl* , is described; it is this we see Ragnar explaining to Rollo in Season 1. This was used for determining latitude, by measuring the height of the sun over the horizon at noon. It was a circular wooden board about ten to twelves inches in diameter with a gnomon, or pointer, at its center, the height of which could be set to the time of the year (as the sun is lower in the sky at noon in the winter than the summer). To keep it level, the board was floated in a bucket of water. Next, the shadow of the noon sun was observed. A concentric circle on the board gave the line the shadow should reach if the ship was on the desired latitude. If the shadow was beyond the line, the ship was north of this latitude; if inside, the ship was south of it.

If the noonday shadow reached the same circle, you could be sure you were going due east or west. Of course, you needed to know when noon was, so you should start making measurements "around noon" and start marking the position of the shadow on the board. The point where the shadow is shortest, and hence the sun is highest in the sky, would be noon. This form of open-water navigation would not be improved on until the invention of the marine chronometer in the eighteenth century, and accurate fixes on a ship's position would not become available until scientific radio and GPS systems became available in the twentieth century.

The final method of navigation we mention in Season 1 was, until recently, a little more contentious. One of the sagas, *Rauðúlfs Tale*, mentions an incident that must have been typical of northerly voyages. Navigation requires knowing where the sun is; under leaden, snowy skies, this can be tricky. When King Olaf asked the hero Sigurd to manage this feat in the saga, Sigurd grabbed a "sun stone" and correctly estimated where the sun must be by looking through it to see the invisible disk of the sun.

Just what this sun stone is has long baffled historians and it has often been dismissed as a "magical" narrative device. However, archaeologists have noted for some time that some forms of calcite, notably Iceland spar, may variably polarize light, depending on the orientation of the crystal. At one particular point, however, known as the "isotropy point," the crystal eliminates all polarization. This property was exploited recently by physicists at the University of Rennes 1 in France; the scientists noted that, at this point, if the calcite is suddenly removed from the line of sight, a faint yellow streak known as Haidinger's Brush is briefly visible. This polarization artifact in the eye rather conveniently points directly toward where the hidden sun is.

No Iceland spar has been found in Viking nautical contexts, but, after Season 1 had aired, a piece of Icelandic spar that might well be a sun stone was discovered on a Tudor shipwreck in the English channel—a hint, perhaps, at the antiquity of Ragnar's technique.

THE STORY OF
FLOKI

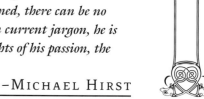

Just like the god Loki, Floki is a shipbuilder and a joker. A pagan fundamentalist, he is alarmed when his close friend Ragnar appears to develop a genuine interest in Christianity and the Christian God. As far as Floki is concerned, there can be no reconciliation between Thor's Hammer and Christ's Cross. In current jargon, he is probably bipolar, but the description does no justice to the heights of his passion, the depths of his despair.

—MICHAEL HIRST

Floki represents the heart of Viking culture yet he remains an outsider. A devout believer in the Norse gods, he is, at one level, as Viking as it is possible to be. However, Floki's quick mind and his mischievous cynicism also place him on the outskirts of his society, from where he can dream of new worlds and new wonders. Like the god Loki, he is both an integral part of Viking life and also its potential nemesis.

The connection between Loki and Floki had been a key theme when Michael Hirst was developing his character, and elements from Loki's mythology often appear in Floki's life. When Floki and Helga have a daughter, he insists on calling the child Angrboða. According to the *Poetic Edda* and the *Prose Edda*, Angrboða, whose name means "she who brings grief," was a *jötunn*, or a giantess who had several children with the god Loki. The Eddas differ on exactly which children she had with him, but the *Prose Edda* states that their children were: Fenrir, the monstrous wolf who will kill Odin during Ragnarök; Jörmungandr, the World Serpent, who will kill (and be killed by) Thor at Ragnarök; and Hel, who presides over the dead in Hel.

Angrboða represents the mother of the creatures who will bring about the end of the current world—a fairly frightening image. We don't have much detail on her beyond this, although one tale suggests that Loki, having eaten Angrboða's heart, bore the three children.

Loki is also credited as the father of various other supernatural creatures. By his wife Sigyn he was the father of Narfi and Nari (possibly just one, although they may be the same person). Stranger still, Loki was the mother to Odin's eight-legged horse Sleipnir, having taken the form of a mare.

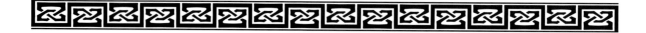

OPPOSITE: Gustaf Skarsgård as Floki.

GUSTAF SKARSGÅRD (FLOKI): Before playing Floki, I read a lot of books about the old religion and the way they lived. It was important for me to understand their view of the world, how different it is from ours today. Their belief, their morals, their code, so different and very fascinating! I have always been interested in the period, and have heard a lot of the old sagas as a child, so I was very grateful of this opportunity to really dive into it and learn more. I think being a modern Scandinavian also helps—I am a Viking.

Floki's main conflict in Season 3 is that he is torn between his loyalty to Ragnar and to his gods. He does not agree with Ragnar's flirtation with Christianity. It actually terrifies him. He feels he has to do whatever necessary to save his dear friend and all of their futures from such heretic behavior and the wrath of the gods.

Spending so much time in the ninth century has totally altered my perception of the time. I'm way more fascinated by it now. The complexity of the society, the relationships, their view of the world. And especially their magic and their mysticism. Pretty far from the stereotypical, ax-swinging wild man. Even though we do swing a lot of axes as well . . .

JOAN BERGIN (COSTUME DESIGNER): We feel we know Floki the boatbuilder by now, but Gustaf works hard to constantly surprise us. We do not always agree at the start but when the big Floki smile lights up his face at the completed look, there are hugs all around in the dressing room.

Floki's leather tunic is a thing of rare beauty. The tunic design is achieved by tooling leather over a tree bark and some leaves. It was made by Liam Rodden, our tailor. For Season 3, Kelvin Feeny, our accessories and prop maker, wove an extraordinary collar from a Viking basket design with matching arm pieces and cuffs to enhance Floki as both boatbuilder and fearless warrior.

GUSTAF SKARSGÅRD (FLOKI): I'm always very involved in choosing the look for my characters. It's a big part of my job. The makeup artist Tom McInerney and I have a great collaboration. He is such a talent and we have a lot of fun playing with Floki's look. The same goes for the costume designer, Joan Bergin, and her lovely staff. The look being so extreme certainly helps me to get into character.

TOM McINERNEY (CHIEF MAKEUP ARTIST): In *Vikings* we've taken license with our interpretation of paganism. We know from the tenth-century writings of Ibn Fadlan that both Viking men and women wore eye makeup to enhance their beauty. Floki's makeup is an homage to what we conceive to be a pagan ceremonial celebration of ritualism and beautification. And Floki's makeup doesn't stop at the eyes. He has quite an elaborate look, and each part of it helps tell his story, much as the tattoos do for the other cast.

JIL TURNER (SET DECORATOR): Floki, we know from the script, is a boatbuilder and has a bit of shaman in him. His house was one of my favorites to dress. We built his bed and table in the shape of a boat. Because of his fascination with trees and wood, I had a huge tree hanging upside down so all that was visible were the gnarled roots.

ABOVE: Shipbuilder, warrior, and joker, Floki owes much to his near namesake, the trickster god Loki.
OPPOSITE: The true believer. Floki fights for the old religion he feels is ebbing away.

VIKING WEDDINGS

Marriages usually took place on Friday, the day of Frigga, the goddess of marriage. In much of the Viking world, due to weather conditions, marriages could also only take place in summer.

Before the wedding itself, the bride symbolically would leave behind her old life and prepare for the new life. This involved taking a steam bath—a sort of early sauna—to wash away her old status before being dressed in new clothes. Later in Scandinavian history, unmarried girls wore a circlet on their heads that was replaced with a bridal crown, usually a family heirloom, when they married. We don't know if Viking girls did this, but it may well date from this period.

According to the sagas, the Viking groom was required to produce an ancestral item, usually a sword, to demonstrate his family lineage and emphasize the fame of his predecessors. This might be a weapon that was already in his family, perhaps owned by a relative, or, failing that, the groom might break open the burial mound of an ancestor and take his sword from there.

For the wedding itself, the bride wore her hair down—the last time she would do so—and both bride and groom wore new clothes, although neither was specifically a bridal outfit. The ceremony probably took place outside, starting with religious invocations and perhaps a sacrifice. Blood from the sacrificed animal would then be sprinkled on the couple. The groom would present his ancestral sword to his new wife, and she would present him with a sword that she had brought for him. This represented the coming together of the two families. Finger rings were sometimes exchanged, and an oath might be taken on an arm ring in a local temple or at a temporary altar.

OPPOSITE TOP: The marriage is sealed with an exchange of swords.
OPPOSITE BOTTOM: Floki and Helga (Maude Hirst) on their wedding day.
FOLLOWING SPREAD: Judith (Jennie Jacques) journeying to Wessex with her father King Aelle (Ivan Kaye).

PART TWO:
ENGLAND

CHRISTIAN ENGLAND

 will bring evil from the north, and a great destruction. The lion is come up from his thicket, and the destroyer of the Gentiles is on his way; he is gone forth from his place to make thy land desolate; and thy cities shall be laid waste, without an inhabitant . . .

— JEREMIAH, 4:6-7

IN EPISODE 3 OF SEASON I ("DISPOSSESSED"), we re-created an actual scene recorded in the *Chronicle of Aethelweard* for the year 789, which marked the first appearance of the Vikings on English soil, some four years before the famous attack on the monastery at Lindisfarne. In our version, Ragnar and his band land on the beach and are met by the reeve (from which we get the word "sheriff"— "shire reeve"), the local king's representative. The *Chronicle* has this scene take place in Wessex, which we transposed to Northumbria; the tense scene of misunderstandings and frail truces seemed to perfectly characterize the clash of cultures that was about to occur. It was a scene that would end in bloodshed.

One of the surviving manuscripts of the *Anglo-Saxon Chronicle* adds that these Vikings were from the region of Hörthaland, in Norway, and the England they had landed in was one of a group of Anglo-Saxon kingdoms that had emerged in the late fifth and sixth centuries, after the collapse of Roman rule. We call these kingdoms "Anglo-Saxon" after the two Germanic tribes, the Angles and Saxons, some of whom migrated to Britain in this period. Theirs was an overwhelmingly agricultural land—a land of scattered farmsteads and small villages in a landscape dominated by forests that had actually increased in size since the end of the Roman period. In the south, three great forests—Andredeswald in the east, the central Ashdown Forest, and Selwood in the west—covered much of the land and were still home to wolves, wild boar, and beavers. Between these dangerous obstacles lay upland pastures on which sheep, goats, and cattle grazed; pannage (wild foraging areas) for pigs; and the lowland fields in which the staples of Anglo-Saxon life— wheat, barley, oats, and rye—were grown.

The people of this place were mostly poor farmers growing enough for their own families to eat and perhaps a little more besides to sell. At the bottom of the scale lay the slaves, who even at the time of the Norman Conquest still formed 10 percent of the population generally and up to 25 percent in some areas. These people were the workhorses of this agricultural world, the men often working in plow teams and the women as dairy maids, although some slaves might be trained in more delicate crafts, such as goldsmithing.

Above the slaves were those granted freedom by their owners, often in a will. Then came the largest category of all, the free peasants, or *ceorls*, who while not necessarily wealthy had their freedom. In return for that freedom, the free peasants bore the duties of public service and taxation, along with the right to participate in local courts. Above this, we enter the ranks of nobility and the world of the landowning classes, the *thegn*, which literally means "the one who serves," although in the *thegn*'s case this service was to the king rather than the people. These individuals, usually but not always men, had local power and influence; they also had a place at court and were the vital link between king and country. They could be officers in the royal household, helping to run the administration, they might be friends or relatives of the king, and they would certainly be expected to answer the royal call to battle. But they were also the most important people in each district, connected to the local social network and thus able to take the king's commands into the countryside and down from the court to the level of the ordinary man and woman. When the king called for money or fighting men, he relied on the *thegns* to ensure that his words were not just heard but acted upon. Foremost among these men stood the *Ealdormen*, men capable of raising whole armies and hence of making or breaking a kingdom.

Although this was a society that had largely adopted Christianity in the seventh century, it was still one that rarely "turned the other cheek." Warfare between these kingdoms, and between dynasties within them, was considered a perfectly normal part of political life, and the bloody feats of warriors were still lauded in the Anglo-Saxon poetry regularly recited in the lord's hall. Although written laws existed, the blood feud was still an important part of justice. Every man and woman of every rank had a price—alive, dead, or variously maimed—and an attacker was required to pay the individual (or relatives, in the case of murder) that "blood price." Failure to do so could result in a feud where cheated relatives might legally exact their own bloody revenge on the culprit. It was not, in this respect, much different from the Viking society it was about to so physically collide with.

But although times were still violent, and folk memories of pagan times lingered on in Saxon songs and stories, Christianity had changed the mindset of these people. In their Christian worldview, God was everywhere, able to intercede on behalf of believers and punish those who strayed from the true path. This was a time when saints were not just stories but real living men and women, when miracles really seemed to happen. God heard and saw all, and an oath made in His name was the highest law in the land. Now they were about to face an enemy who simply didn't believe in their God or the terrible sanctity of His oath. Worse than that, for the Christian Anglo-Saxons, the arrival of the Vikings was not simply an unfortunate increase in piracy—it was the fulfilling of an Old Testament prophecy. In their minds, this marked the beginning of the end of the world.

CHAPTER
8

CHRISTIANS

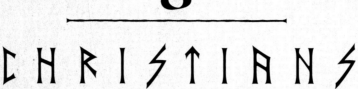

ATHELSTAN ON ENGLAND IN DARKNESS:

THE DARKNESS THAT NOW DESCENDS ON THE WORLD of the Christians is of our own making, for we have strayed from the path of righteousness. This is what our Holy Father tells us. The end of the world is almost upon us, just as the biblical prophet Jeremiah warned, when he said:

"Out of the north an evil shall break forth upon all the inhabitants of the land."

But we know from those who wrote our history, from the monk they called Bede, that it was not always this way in the lands of the English. Across the country we still see the wracked ruins of great cities and palaces, places the simple people fear to enter, believing them inhabited by the ghosts of those they call "the giants." We who read know these were the homes of the Romans who once ruled this land and who brought great wealth and prosperity. Then there were many people, crowded into towns, and travelers from across the world brought rare treasures to trade. This was a Christian place when the Romans repented the murder of Our Lord, and happy we were to bend to their will and accept their protection.

But all this has turned to dust. Pavements are smashed, roofs have fallen. The Romans left to fight barbarians who teemed over the borders of their empire and they never returned. In their wake, pagan people swarmed across this country, bringing darkness. Only one man stood against them, whom some call Arthur but whom the learned know as Ambrosius Aurelianus, but he could not hold back the tide forever. And the Word of the Lord was silenced in all but the distant places of the west, and the books were destroyed and learning forgotten.

Then the people lived like animals, scrabbling in the dirt, and those who once lived in great halls cowered in low, wooden huts. Men who once commanded great estates lived themselves like slaves. The country was split into warring kingdoms, and blood flowed like water in the rivers, until salvation came. For Pope Gregory, in distant Rome, saw slaves of the English tribe they called Angles in the market there and declared them not Angles but Angels and sent the Blessed St. Augustine to restore the faith to our shores.

It was Augustine who taught the kings to turn from their pretended gods and embrace the true faith. With his words, peace returned and men built churches again, and parents brought their children to the monastery doors, asking that they become monks. Once again people looked out across the sea to other lands, and traders came with fine goods from far away, and those who lived in lands that had also belonged to the Romans joined hands with us in fellowship.

But men are weak, and the temptations of sin are strong. How quickly we forgot the blessings the church had brought us, and how soon we reverted to our base ways. Even though the Holy Father warned us that the Last Days were almost upon us, we preferred easy living and luxury, and fell to greedy squabbling. And so the Northmen arrived. And the prophecy of Jeremiah came to pass. As our brother Alcuin has said:

Behold, Judgment has begun.

DESIGNING LINDISFARNE

The monks of Lindisfarne were quite different from later medieval monastics. Their traditions were ancient and homegrown, or at least date from much earlier Roman forms of Christianity. Biographies of saints from Lindisfarne comment on their love of nature, particularly birds and animals, and their preference for a very simple life. When St. Cuthbert, their most revered saint and abbot, retired, he went to live entirely alone on an island in a single stone cell where he could dedicate himself to contemplating God's creation.

But these monks weren't simply hermits. Their religion encouraged them to travel, and they often undertook pilgrimages and missions abroad. At a time when the vast majority of the population was illiterate, many of the monks were well-read and had access to excellent libraries as well as frequent correspondence with the outside world.

The raid on their monastery in AD 793 changed much of this lifestyle, marking as it does one of the first appearances of Viking war bands who would from now on prey on undefended monastic sites. The *Anglo-Saxon Chronicle* for the year sets the tone:

In this year dire forewarnings came over the land of the Northumbrians, and miserably terrified the people: there were excessive whirlwinds and lightning, and fiery dragons were seen flying in the air. A great famine soon followed these tokens; and a little after that, in the same year, on the VIth of the Ides of January, the havoc of the heathen men miserably destroyed God's church at Lindisfarne, through rapine and slaughter.

This text provided the inspiration for the *Vikings* scene that takes place the night before Ragnar's ship arrives, when the monks of Lindisfarne cower in fear of the electrical storm outside, seeing "fiery dragons" in the changing shapes of clouds. During the raid itself, we could also show the attack from the Viking perspective, for a change. While the monks believed the Vikings were the scourge of God, the Vikings themselves couldn't understand how such treasures could be left unprotected in the hands of unarmed monks.

The monastery of Lindisfarne did, in fact, survive the raid of 793. In 875, however, the Vikings took the monastery, and the monks fled, never to return.

ABOVE: Gold and jewels used in Christian devotion lured Viking raiders to these poorly defended sites.
OPPOSITE: Concept art for the attack on Lindisfarne.
PREVIOUS SPREAD: Monastic scriptoria were famed for their elaborate manuscript decorations.

TOM CONROY (PRODUCTION DESIGNER): For the monastery interiors and exteriors, we adapted an old farmstead lying somewhat inland—dressing sand dunes on the outside of the defensive walls and allowing "windblown" sand to cover the courtyards, to give the illusion of being near the sea.

The interior walls were whitewashed—so it feels very different and quite a contrast to the Viking homes. The light bounces in from the sandy courtyards. You see frescoes being painted on the walls. There were illuminated manuscripts— so for once there are intense colors . . . And then there are treasures—bejeweled candelabras, chalices, and tabernacles, all brighter than we have seen in the Viking world so far.

JIL TURNER (SET DECORATOR): In the monastery of Lindisfarne, and on the Anglo-Saxon sets in general, I tried to show the contrast of the different cultures through the furnishings, fabrics, and food.

For instance, I commissioned two types of bread— Viking flatbread and a more rustic, oval-shaped loaf for the Saxons. These subtle details I felt would subliminally help the audience believe the clash of cultures.

The monastery set is as stark as it is orderly and structured. It shows a clearly settled and organized group that prays to a different God. This manifests itself through the repetition of stylistic elements in their work area, dormitory area, in the bedding, the lighting, and their seating/dining hall. When the Vikings land, they appear to be more brutish and wild, while the monks are ordered in their setting.

BILL HALLIDAY (VFX PRODUCER): The dragon-cloud shot in the episode "The Wrath of the Northmen," where Athelstan sees the vision of the dragon in the sky prior to the Vikings' attack on Lindisfarne, was done using stock footage of clouds, which we then manipulated as a matte painting to form the dragon shape.

ABOVE: Athelstan works in the scriptorium of Lindisfarne.

THE STORY OF
ATHELSTAN

Athelstan is a young Christian monk who is captured during the first Viking raid on Lindisfarne monastery. Carried back to Scandinavia to be sold as a slave, Athelstan attracts Ragnar's attention because he tried to save not some rich and precious object, but a book: the Gospels. Athelstan becomes part of Ragnar's household, and eventually even goes raiding with him back to England, but throughout, he suffers a spiritual crisis, a man of faith torn between two cultures.

—MICHAEL HIRST

Some of what we know about monks like Athelstan comes from the surviving letters of a real contemporary monk, Alcuin. Alcuin had been a scholar at the monastic school at York in the later part of the eighth century, where his work had come to the attention of Charlemagne, who tempted him away to run the famous Palace School at the Carolingian court. Charlemagne's school was considered the most civilized, cultured, and literate place in northern Europe, but Alcuin's letters show that this golden age of learning in England and Frankia was coming under threat as the age of Viking attacks approached.

The terrifying Anglo-Saxon poem known as "Christ III" describes the scene at the Day of Judgment: The stars are scattered, the moon falls from the sky, the sun dims and dies, and the world is illuminated only by the light from a bloodstained cross. To religious men like Alcuin, the beginnings of Viking raids looked eerily like the opening shots of that Judgment Day. These Vikings were not simply a nuisance or an insult; they were a punishment from God, the fulfillment of an ancient prophecy, and the herald of the end of time itself. On hearing of the Lindisfarne attack, Alcuin immediately wrote to the King Ethelred of Northumbria, warning that there was more to this than just chance:

"Consider carefully, brothers, and examine diligently, lest perchance this unaccustomed and unheard-of evil was merited by some unheard-of evil practice."

Intriguingly, in a letter to the bishop of Lindisfarne, Alcuin does indicate some apparent contact between the pagan raiders and the court of his master, Charlemagne. He promises, when he next sees the emperor, to bring up the issue of the "youths taken into captivity," by which he seems to mean the young monks taken into slavery during the Lindisfarne raid. Clearly, Alcuin thinks that Charlemagne may be able to exert influence on either the raiders or the rulers of their homelands to get the young monks returned.

This episode in history provided the genesis for the character of Athelstan, who bridges two worlds. Athelstan is one who, as he says in Season 1, has traveled; so, for all his monastic naïveté, he knows more of the world outside than many a Viking. In an era when we think of people as rarely straying farther than a few miles from home, it is this ability to survive in alien cultures and learn from them that so intrigues two men—Ragnar and Ecbert—who both would also like to know more of the wider world.

GEORGE BLAGDEN (ATHELSTAN): Michael told me at the start of Season 1 that he had based Athelstan on a real historical figure, a monk who had been captured by the Vikings at Lindisfarne monastery and taken back to Scandinavia as a slave. I took a research trip to Lindisfarne Island, and learned a lot about the devout way of life that the monks lived in this very isolated community. But in terms of approaching this complex character, we didn't actually know that Athelstan was going to be all that complex! Michael didn't allow the actors to see scripts too far in advance, which meant that the complexity of his character was built into the story without my being able to prepare for it too much. It meant that his confusion, once presented with the alien world of the Vikings, was a lot more organic.

I remember a scene in Season 1 where Athelstan was listening to Floki at a fireside talking about how the Vikings believed the world had been created. I (George) hadn't learned anything about that beforehand, and I think it is probably where I am most happy with my acting in the entire show, because I can see in the take that Athelstan is actually listening to Floki tell him a story. No acting required.

LINUS ROACHE (KING ECBERT): Ecbert is fascinated by Athelstan because he has actually lived and absorbed the Viking culture and can appreciate more than one worldview. Ecbert has rarely met anyone who agrees with him who is not a sycophant. He sees Athelstan as the son he wishes he had and he truly loves him in an almost unreasonable, possessive way, wanting his allegiance more than anyone else's because that would be the greatest personal affirmation for Ecbert.

JIL TURNER (SET DECORATOR): The monk Athelstan's illuminated gospel was a hero prop, so I commissioned seven leather-bound versions of the Gospels from a traditional bookbinder in County Kerry, Ireland. These were done in three stages to reflect the varying time spans of our story. When we first see the Book of Gospels, Athelstan has smuggled it from the monastery in near-perfect condition. In the very last stage, he retrieves the book from under the floorboards, and it disintegrates in his hands. I had commissioned seven copies, as our actors were generally close to water and I was certain that we would lose some to the sea! Luckily, this never came to pass.

ABOVE: Apostate. Athelstan joins the Viking war band.
OPPOSITE TOP: Athelstan and Ragnar form an unlikely but powerful alliance.
OPPOSITE BOTTOM: Born again. Athelstan rediscovers his Christian beliefs.

DRESSING ATHELSTAN

Athelstan undergoes a series of psychological and physical transformations over the first three seasons of Vikings, from monk to slave to warrior and back again, as he is forced to accept, then willingly embraces, a new culture and religion before returning to the beliefs and society of his youth. This transformation in character was mirrored in the costuming of Athelstan.

JOAN BERGIN (COSTUME DESIGNER): With that beatific face, the monk was easy. It is one of my favorite character transitions in the series even if difficult to achieve. I felt it important that Athelstan's conversion be no sudden, superhero costume with all axes blazing.

Instead, it should hint at a note of ambiguity. Wonderfully, the actor gave that anyway, and the costume was one of his props.

GEORGE BLAGDEN (ATHELSTAN): With the number of different looks that Athelstan has to go through during the course of the three seasons, it made it easier to take elements from his look to help with his character. I didn't have much choice about the shaved circle on his head, though.

DEE CORCORAN (CHIEF HAIR DESIGNER): As much as George wasn't looking forward to his tonsure, he was very professional in understanding the historical significance of the look and the importance for his character in having the contrasting hairstyles as he converts from monk to Viking. Interesting to note that Athelstan has had more hairstyles than most of the female characters in the show!

GEORGE BLAGDEN (ATHELSTAN): I'm not sure what I like most about Athelstan—I suppose his amazing ability to survive in any situation. But I *definitely* dislike his tonsure the most.

ABOVE: George Blagden as Athelstan.
OPPOSITE: Monk, slave, warrior. Athelstan's costume has to convey a huge emotional journey.

THE HEAT OF BATTLE

SEASON 3, EPISODE 2: "THE WANDERER"

In Season 3, Episode 2 ("The Wanderer"), we witness the major engagement between the Vikings, aided by Princess Kwenthrith, and the Mercians under King Brihtwulf. This provided an opportunity to show the physical, personal nature of warfare in the ninth century—in particular, with the death of Brihtwulf, distracted by a fly and cut down by Floki. In the wounding of Torstein, one of Ragnar's most trusted friends and raiding partners, it also enabled us to show how even a small wound in battle could become a death sentence in an age before antiseptics and antibiotics.

It also gave us the opportunity to show the details of Viking warfare. Fighting was a part of everyday Viking life, and the tools of war were often also the tools for everyday jobs. The only real exception to this was the sword—generally only carried by professional warriors.

The main weapon of the period for Viking and Anglo-Saxon alike was the spear. This was Odin's weapon, which he threw down to earth to start wars. Another easily accessible weapon was the ax, which at this date was usually an agricultural tool with a two- to three-foot handle and a three- to six-inch iron blade.

The majority of Vikings had no proper armor. Coats of mail made of interlinked iron rings were available to the very wealthy, but, for most, a padded jacket was all they could hope for. Wealthy warriors might afford an iron helmet—but there is not a single piece of archaeological or historical evidence that any Viking ever had horns on his helmet.

The standard battle formation of the period was the shield wall—in which opposing divisions confronted each other with a rank of interlocked shields. The armies would then advance toward each other and probe the enemy's defenses using their spears, jabbing through the gaps. Among the Vikings, it was the honor of the youngest fighters to take their position in the front rank of the shield wall with the more experienced warriors behind them.

But Viking tactics were not simply about might. Viking war bands generally tried to avoid battle; indeed, the key to their success was their ability to strike where least expected and then disappear again before battle lines could be drawn. There was no dishonor for a Viking to retreat if it meant surviving to fight another day, and, faced with a superior force, Viking war bands often simply left the field. Feigned retreat was also a useful tactic and one that the Normans, descendants of the Viking Rollo, used to win the Battle of Hastings in 1066.

KEN GIROTTI (DIRECTOR): Michael writes battle scenes that are essential to the storytelling. In other words, the battles themselves are small stories. So, part of the end of the big battle in Episode 7 of Season 1 is all about Floki's anger at Rollo, and Rollo trying to make things right with the gods by killing as many Christians as he can (whether they're already dead or not). There's more weight to this than a simple slashfest.

The other thing has to do with simple military tactics and maneuvers. The big battle in Episode 9 of Season 2 is all about Horik deciding that what will happen is fated by the gods, but Ragnar sees it differently; perhaps he feels he can influence fate. However, he is bound to follow his king into battle. And the superior tactics of King Ecbert reign supreme. He has his horsemen fight in ways the Vikings have never seen. The soldiers on horseback don't dismount and fight as the Vikings would expect; they simply ride into the shield wall and tear it apart. Plus, Ecbert has the Saxon attack come from three fronts. The Vikings are used to standing up to

frontal assaults, nothing else. The attack from three fronts deals the Vikings their first defeat in the course of the series.

With story, the battles have meaning, and the players have stakes!

P.J. DILLON (DIRECTOR OF PHOTOGRAPHY): The show's various directors plan and storyboard the battle sequences very carefully. I usually get involved in this process at an early stage so that we can examine the logistics involved in bringing the directors' ideas to the screen. Each battle has its own unique motif. For example, the first battle scene in Season 3 involves a beach landing, so we shot a lot of it in water. This naturally involved challenges not normally encountered in land-based battles, so we had to adapt our shooting style accordingly. My main task is then to make sure the scenes maintain a visual continuity, while the directors are watching to make sure the individual beats all add up to a compelling scene that makes narrative sense.

ABOVE: Floki ponders the value of a crown.
OPPOSITE: A wooden wall of shields was the only defense in battle.
FOLLOWING SPREAD: Viking battles were fought hand to hand and at close quarters, requiring huge physical strength.

CHAPTER
9

KINGS

KING ECBERT ON THE AGE OF GIANTS:

OUR LAND IS FILLED WITH MEMORIES of distant times, memories of other people who lived here long ago. There are stones from a time before books, before learning, that have stood watch on the plains since the beginning of time. And there are the ruins built by greater people, giants perhaps, who in ancient times heaped up vast cities from stone.

This was the age of the Romans, when Britain was rich and prosperous and the countryside was filled with palaces and great mansions whose floors were decorated with intricate mosaics—more beautiful than those I saw at the mighty Charlemagne's court. The ruins of these grand mansions still lie scattered in the wilderness, their fields overgrown and their owners sleeping deep in the soil.

I cannot say why the Romans left, but other people came, and our monks preserve a book from those dark days when all learning fell into abeyance and violence ruled. Gildas the Wise lived in those times and wrote of their history in his book *The Ruin of Britain*, which tells us that when the Saxons invaded, one Roman, Ambrosius Aurelianus, gathered together his men and stood against the invaders. He defeated them in the great battle of Mons Badonicus. Alas, his victory was squandered by those who came after him.

Then the world fell into darkness, and all learning and love of Christ was lost until the blessed St. Augustine came to these shores on the divine inspiration of the Holy Father Gregory. The monks tell us that Gregory was walking in the markets of Rome and saw some fair-skinned slaves for sale. When he asked who they were, he was told they were Angles from England. The saint replied in the tongue of the Romans: "*Non Angli, sed Angeli*"—"not Angles but angels"—and was at that moment inspired to send Augustine to be our apostle.

So, slowly, the light has returned to these shores; still, the glimmer is slight, and we still live in the shadow of the Age of Giants.

DESIGNING KING ECBERT'S COURT

Although Winchester was nominally the "capital" of Wessex, the royal court at this date had no permanent base but traveled around the country from royal estate to royal estate. This wandering existence was a necessary part of managing royal property, ensuring that law and order, such as they were, were maintained while keeping a reasonably firm control on those great lords whom the king relied upon to administer his kingdom.

To create one of these "vills" (the central settlement and administrative center in each rural territory), we took inspiration from a surviving anonymous poem of the period, "The Ruin," in which the poet describes himself walking through the shattered remains of a Roman town or fortress.

> *Wondrous is this masonry, shattered by the Fates.*
> *The fortifications have given way, the buildings raised by*
> *giants are crumbling. The roofs have collapsed; the*
> *towers are in ruins. There is rime on the mortar. The*
> *walls are rent and broken away, and have fallen, under-*
> *mined by age. The owners and builders are perished and*
> *gone, and have been held fast in the earth's embrace, the*
> *ruthless clutch of the grave, while a hundred generations*
> *of mankind have passed away.*

TOM CONROY (PRODUCTION DESIGNER): To me this was like a key to a treasure chest. We talked about an ancient palace, still intact enough to hold a thermal bath. It would have staterooms and reception rooms and large courtyards and would be in a big enough setting to show the power and wealth of this kingdom. We can see that Ragnar is up against a formidable and sophisticated foe.

We built studio sets of the baths, reception rooms, and more private quarters. The bath was designed to fit up to a dozen people, surrounded with beautiful, if decayed, frescos. I happily volunteered to be the first to test it! We adapted an old stone building as a central courtyard of the Roman palace, with the VFX team providing the set extensions.

LINUS ROACHE (KING ECBERT): It's actually nice in the bath. The water is warm. As an aspiring actor, I used to say that I did some of my best work in the bath—and now I get to be in the bath on set! So I have no excuses. Playing a man so obsessed with our Roman history has also given me much greater respect for it and how culture is constantly evolving as we learn from the success and failures of the past.

ABOVE: Ecbert holds court as ruler of Wessex.
OPPOSITE: Concept art for Ecbert's bathhouse.
PREVIOUS SPREAD: King Ecbert of Wessex (Linus Roache) prays for deliverance.

ROMAN BRITAIN

The Anglo-Saxons of the eighth century came from a world where building in stone was almost unknown, so the ruins of Roman cities and villas that they found scattered across the country seemed to them to belong to a legendary time when giants inhabited the land—for who else could have built such vast structures? These remnants also seemed impossibly ancient but, in truth it was only a few hundred years since the lost world described by the writer of "The Ruin" had been the thriving Roman spa city of Bath. There is a good chance that his ancestors once walked in those streets. There is also a chance that it was his ancestors who brought them to ruin.

Although Julius Caesar had visited Britain in 55 and 54 BC, it was the emperor Claudius who ordered the invasion in AD 43. From that time on, Britannia became a Roman province—and remained so until the fifth century, when the removal of the legions and the arrival of the Anglo-Saxons from continental Europe is said to mark the beginning of the "Dark Ages." The term "Dark Ages," in truth, has more to do with how brightly the Victorians imagined the classical world (and their own) to shine, rather than how dimly remembered this time

actually was, or how ignorant its people. No doubt the world of Sub-Roman Britain, as this time is now known, was a far cry from the days when Britain was a Roman province, but Rome had not suddenly abandoned Britain; rather, it had mutated and faded away over centuries. For the large-scale villa owners who exploited great rural estates in Roman Britain, the good times might have drawn to a close, but for the small farmer, for whom Rome was mostly another tax burden, life had not really changed.

As they drifted back into many of their pre-Roman ways, now infused with the culture and legends of Germanic European arrivals, the people of Britain largely slipped from written history. The brief glimpse of names and faces we gained during the Roman occupation is again clouded as literacy is largely forgotten. The British would emerge again in the seventh and eighth centuries, transformed into the people of the Anglo-Saxon kingdoms of England—the people who would now face the fury of the Vikings.

THE STORY OF
KING ECBERT

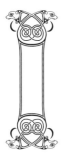

Ecbert is to the Saxon world what Ragnar is to the Viking world—an original. He spent part of his youth at the glittering court of the emperor Charlemagne, so he knows about politics and power. And he uses his knowledge, becoming king of Wessex and planning to become bretwalda, *king of kings, king of all England. He will use everyone and everything in the cause of his ambition, including the Vikings. But his relationship with both Ragnar and Athelstan puts a new twist on his story.*

—MICHAEL HIRST

England at the time of our series was not one country but a series of small kingdoms, today called the heptarchy—after the seven major kingdoms of Northumbria, Mercia, East Anglia, Essex, Kent, Sussex, and Wessex. The kingdom of the West Saxons (known as Wessex) was centered in the south and west of England and expanded during the reign of Ecbert and his successors—particularly Alfred the Great—until it absorbed many of the other kingdoms.

There was a real Ecbert. His accession to the throne of Wessex in the year 802 began the transformation of that nation, and his descendants would go on to become the first kings of England. Until that time, the state of Mercia had dominated much of southern England. After Ecbert's defeat of the Mercians at the battle of Ellunden in 825 and his subsequent invasion of their territory, he became the overlord of the heptarchy—the greatest among those kings and their overlord—known as a *bretwalda* in Anglo-Saxon. At the time we meet him he is the most powerful ruler in the British Isles, capable not only of influencing the decisions of other kings but also of imposing his will on a government (known as a *witan*) that still had the right to depose him. When Ecbert dies, it will be his son who succeeds him—not a foregone conclusion in Anglo-Saxon politics up to this point in time—marking the birth of one of the greatest British royal dynasties.

LINUS ROACHE (KING ECBERT): Based on the limited facts known about Ecbert there was a lot of scope to create a character who was a politician and a diplomat as much as a warrior king, and also a man of great ambition and vision. I like to think of Ecbert as the founding father of the British monarchy.

Of course one does all the research one can about the period and the culture, but in the end it's about inhabiting a character. Most of my preparation now is about exploring the many dimensions of what Michael Hirst puts on the page and making sure I don't limit the potential of what is nearly always there right in front of me.

The most fun scene for me in Season 3 was in Episode 5

["The Usurper"], where Ecbert berates his court and his son for acting without his consent—and then you discover he was actually behind the raid on the Viking settlement, and it was all a bluff. It was a great moment of flipping things around and revealing Ecbert's true nature and real intention, which had been hidden up till then. The reveal in Episode 5 was a relief. Finally, I could let the cat out of the bag.

KATHERYN WINNICK (LAGERTHA): I really enjoyed working with Linus Roache in our scenes together this past season. I think King Ecbert brought a different side out of her, more playful yet inquisitive.

OPPOSITE: Ecbert and Lagertha share a love of farming.

JOAN BERGIN (COSTUME DESIGNER): It is always interesting when a figure from long centuries ago presents us with the urbanity, elegance, and political calculation of a modern statesman. Ecbert was a complex, sophisticated man for his era—a man who had lived at the court of Charlemagne—and we sought to explain or show this through the laid-back splendor of his clothes. He rarely wore his crown, loved the color blue and jeweled tunics. He seduced all before him with charm and no small degree of self-interest. One would have liked to have met him.

LINUS ROACHE (KING ECBERT): The sets feel so authentic, and when I walk on wearing King Ecbert's heavy and detailed costume and look around at all the extras, there are moments when I think this must be close to how it actually was twelve hundred years ago. The attention to detail on every level of the production is astounding and it all leads to a feeling of authenticity. It allows you to believe more in what you are doing.

VIKING DEFEAT

SEASON 2, EPISODE 9: "THE CHOICE"

In the Season 2 episode called "The Choice," we come upon Ecbert and Athelstan using a copy of Julius Caesar's *Commentaries on the Gallic War* to find methods for beating the Vikings in battle. The section we chose was from Caesar's account of his attack on the Nervians, who lived in what is now Flanders. It seemed ideal for our purposes as the Nervians were influenced by the Germanic northern tribes whose culture heavily influenced the later Vikings.

We don't have a record of Ecbert actually using this book to help defeat the Vikings but we do know that he and his descendants were some of the first rulers of Saxon England to realize the power of the written word, especially the value of surviving Roman books. This was a nice opportunity to convey that idea while also showing how Ecbert worked on analyzing Viking attacks, as he had seen Charlemagne do in Frankia, and how he developed strategies to beat them.

We know that, after initial defeats, Ecbert did turn his fortunes around with a significant victory in the year 838, when a large Viking naval force and a Cornish army joined forces to attack him. Details of the battle are few, but we know that this time he had a resounding victory. The *Anglo-Saxon Chronicle* joyfully records that "both Cornish and Danes were put to flight." This formed the basis for our battle in the episode "The Choice."

CLIVE STANDEN (ROLLO): I find every new fight sequence just as much of a challenge as the last. The logic of our imagination as a viewer demands that everything we see on screen, however unbelievable, is actually happening—or happened—for real. That's the challenge for me when it comes to stunts and fight sequences. There are too many fight scenes on TV or on film that are choreographed to look like a dance, where the lead characters are almost super-human and somehow come out of the battle entirely unscathed, or the whole thing is filmed with very shaky camera work, so it turns into just a mishmash of body parts and blood splatters. It doesn't move me; I don't "believe" it. And, by and large, I can't invest in it. It's full of sound and fury, but ultimately signifies nothing. I always try to use a fight sequence for a chance to continue telling the story or to show an extra aspect of the character I'm playing. A good fight should drive the story forward, transport the audience into the action with you, so that they too feel the danger, the fear, the aggression. There need to be moments of vulnerability. The audience needs to buy into the idea that, at any time, your character could slip up and be cleaved in half.

OPPOSITE: For all the shock and awe of early Viking attacks, their enemies soon adapted, and there were no easy victories.
FOLLOWING SPREAD: Mercia and Wessex in the ninth century.

CHAPTER
10

RIVALS

PRINCESS KWENTHRITH ON MERCIA AND HER KINGS:

MERCIA IS SURELY THE GREATEST OF THE KINGDOMS of the Saxons in England. Lying in the middle of our island, it stretches from the river Humber in the north to the Kingdom of Wessex in the south and from the mountain fastnesses of Wales in the west to the land of the East Angles and East Saxons.

Mercia was never more powerful than under King Offa, who cut the great ditch that separates our land from the Welsh. Offa was cruel but he was the mightiest among the kings of England and took the title *bretwalda* as a mark of that dignity. It was Offa who cast the young Ecbert out of Wessex and into Frankia.

But Offa, not content in his power, wished himself another Charlemagne and demanded the emperor's daughter for his wife. The emperor looked across the water at this little land and laughed, as did Ecbert, who took shelter in his court and swore one day to be *bretwalda* himself.

Such was the power of Offa in Mercia, however, that before he let slip the reins of his life, he ordered his son should rule in his stead. This is not the way of things among the Saxons. There is no rule to say that a king must be succeeded by his son, but rather it is for the wise men of the *witan* to choose from among the great families of the land. Among our people there are many who might be king. And some who might be queen.

Charlemagne had handed his kingdom to his son Louis, who they called "Pious" for his love of Christ, but Louis could not so easily hand his kingdom to his four sons. They showed their love for their father by raising armies against him and in turn deposing and restoring him as they fought among themselves. Finally they called their father to a truce at Colmar, but, when he came, he found his sons arrayed against him in battle. Betrayed by his own sons and his own troops, Louis was made to kneel in the mud and renounce the throne his father had so hard won. Even today, the Franks call this place Lügenfeld—the Field of Lies.

And so it is in Mercia, where we fall to civil war and where the great families of the land looked to force or guile to seize the throne. As the great scholar Alcuin noted:

"For truly, as I think, that most noble young man has not died for his own sins, but the vengeance for the blood shed by the father has reached the son. For you know very well how much blood his father shed to secure the kingdom on his son. This was not a strengthening of his kingdom but its ruin."

And, all the while, Ecbert, having returned home from Frankia, sits waiting on the throne of Wessex.

Kingdom
of Mercia

Hill of the Ash

Battle

II Viking
Camp

Burgred's Camp

Aethelwulf Camp
& Ambush

King's Brihtwulf Camp

Viking Mid
Way Camp

Royal Villa

Lagertha's Camp

Kingdom
of Wessex

Viking Settlement

THE STORY OF
PRINCESS KWENTHRITH

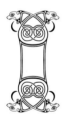

Princess Kwenthrith is a daughter of the House of Mercia, for years the most powerful kingdom in England. Now that kingdom has fallen apart. Brothers and sisters quarrel and fight over the crown. Kwenthrith emerges triumphant because of Ecbert's support, but there is a cost to pay for that support.

— MICHAEL HIRST

The character of Kwenthrith was based on a number of eighth- and ninth-century high-status women who, like their Viking counterparts, took much more of an active role in politics and government than was allowed to the women of the later medieval period. Kwenthrith is partly based on the Mercian princess Cwenthryth— historically, the daughter of King Coenwulf, the successor to Offa's son. She was, however, the sister of St. Kenelm, the Mercian king and martyr, as in the series. According to the Winchcombe legend (a story recorded in a twelfth-century manuscript at Winchcombe Abbey in Gloucestershire, England), Cwenthryth, who coveted the throne, ordered her lover to kill St. Kenelm. Our Kwenthrith also folds in elements of Offa's wife, Cynethryth, an eighth-century Mercian queen and the only Anglo-Saxon woman to have coins minted in her own name, as well as the later Aethelflaed, King Alfred's daughter, who ruled Mercia in the early tenth century and was known as "The Lady of the Mercians."

AMY BAILEY (PRINCESS KWENTHRITH): Kwenthrith is before her time, and has very modern ideas within an old world. Playing her is invigorating, because she is bold and quite fearless. I'd like to think her character has rubbed off and that I might complain about the fly in my soup more readily.

Her reasons for being ruthless are very complex. But there are double standards for Kwenthrith. Men openly display and celebrate their large appetites for sex and power—why the uproar when a woman does?

The poisoning of Kwenthrith's brother Burgred was one of my favorite scenes. Kwenthrith's despair and subsequent resolution about his death mark a shift for the character, because he is the last of her family and her past. It is a horrifying decision because she does love him, but this is a family at war, a family who have already fought her. She knows he'd kill or depose her if he got the chance, so she has no choice. Such is the price of power.

LINUS ROACHE (KING ECBERT): Princess Kwenthrith is an amusement to Ecbert and although she is potentially dangerous he sees her as a wildcat that needs to be contained and controlled but will never be tamed. It almost tickles him to see how scheming she can be. Although it's entertaining, Ecbert knows deep down that ultimately she is no threat to him and that he will always have the upper hand.

OPPOSITE: Amy Bailey as Princess Kwenthrith.
ABOVE: Princess Kwenthrith realizes the cost of revenge.

THE STORY OF
KING AELLE

King Aelle of Northumbria, one of the seven kingdoms of Saxon England, is the unsuspecting host of the first Viking raid on English soil. The attack on the Northumbrian monastery at Lindisfarne goes down in history as the event that announces the Viking age, with all its archetypal features: a peaceful religious community, the sudden appearance of one or more Viking longships, a brutal and murderous attack on unsuspecting monks, the pillaging of holy relics, and the capture of slaves. King Aelle came to power through duplicity and force, but nothing prepared him for dealing with this new threat from the north. His first instinct is to buy off Ragnar and the Northmen, but in the long run Aelle knows that he must come to another solution. And, indeed, his emphatic place in history is a result of this solution.

—MICHAEL HIRST

The King Aelle of *Vikings* is based on a slightly later historical king but one tightly bound up with the story of Ragnar. In AD 858, King Osberht of Northumbria had been ousted by one Aelle whom the Anglo-Saxon chronicler pointedly records as "with no hereditary right." This led to civil war and a financial crisis in which both claimants robbed the Northumbrian people—leading to just the sort of disaffection and division that attracted Vikings to a country.

Of course, the later saga writers could never have so prosaic a reason for Aelle's coming to Viking attention. Their legend has it that Ragnar Lothbrok had met his death at the hands of Aelle, who had thrown him into a snake pit. Initially the snakes refused to touch him, owing to a magical silk shirt he was wearing. But when Aelle noticed this and had it removed, the snakes bit Ragnar; in his dying breath, he prophesied:

"The little pigs would grunt if they knew how it fares with the old boar."

The sagas say that when those "little pigs"—the sons of Ragnar—heard the news, the first son, Hvitserk, who was playing chess at the time, seized a piece so hard that blood oozed from his fingernails, Björn Ironside grabbed a spear with such force that he left an indentation in the wooden shaft, and Sigurd Snake-in-the-Eye, who was trimming his nails, cut clear to the bone. But it was another of the little pigs who would prove the avenger of the tale, legend or not, and that would be Ivar the Boneless.

IVAN KAYE (KING AELLE): At first Aelle believed he was in charge, but, as time passed, the alliance with Ecbert became uneasy. Aelle began to mistrust Ecbert and fear for his control. When Aelle was used as a bargaining tool with the Vikings, his position became more unsteady. Ecbert "seemed" to embrace and entertain the "Viking way," while Aelle feared the transformation in customs. Given the choice, Aelle would have dealt with the Vikings in his own "old-fashioned" style: less guile and more aggression.

My favorite scene to have worked on was when Lord Wigea fails to defend our shores from the Vikings' attack, and is admonished in sinister fashion and dispatched into the snake pit.

LINUS ROACHE (KING ECBERT): Ecbert tolerates King Aelle out of political necessity. He has nothing in common with him and sees him as a mere brute. They are like oil and water. I think Ecbert can't wait for an opportunity to get rid of Aelle.

TRAVIS FIMMEL (RAGNAR LOTHBROK): The thing about knowing your fate as a character is that you can guide your destiny in a way. So I will be sure to give the Saxon kings plenty of reasons to want me dead.

ABOVE: Aelle inspects the Viking battle dead.
OPPOSITE: Ivan Kaye as King Aelle of Northumbria.

RIDDLES

The Anglo-Saxons were a very literate people with a great love of word play, poetry, and, above all, riddles. Riddles provided evening entertainment and were apparently often very bawdy. Many riddles were gathered together in what is today known as the *Exeter Book*, a tenth-century codex containing secular and religious poems and other writings, along with ninety-four riddles. The book was donated to the library of Exeter Cathedral by Leofric, the first bishop of Exeter, in 1072.

The riddles range from poetic to comical to obscene. Meant to be performed rather than merely read to oneself, they give us a glimpse into the life and culture of the era. Here is one of the most famous:

Ic eom wunderlicu wiht wifum on hyhte,
neahbuendum nyt nængum sceþþe
burgsittendra, nymþe bonan anum
stapol min is steapheah stonde ic on bedde
neoþan ruh nathwær neþeð . hwilum
ful cyrtenu . ceorles dohtor
modwlonc meowle þæt heo on me gripeð
ræseð mec on reodne, reafað min heafod
fegeð mec on fæsten feleþ sona
mines gemotes, seo þe mec nearwað
wif wundenlocc Wæt bið þæt eage

I am a wonderful creature, I bring joy to women
And am useful to those nearby; I harm
No one except my destroyer.
My position is high; I stand up in bed;
Beneath, in my hidden place, I am hairy. Sometimes
The beautiful daughter of a poor man,
A courageous girl, will get a grip on me.
She assaults my redness, takes my head,
And holds me tight. She will soon feel
The effect of meeting me, of being near me
This curly-haired woman. Her eye will become wet.

Answer: An onion

VIKINGS IN ENGLAND

There is both archaeological and historical evidence of the Viking incursions and settlements in ninth-century England, and the transition from raiding parties to permanent farmers is one of the long-running themes of *Vikings*.

Saxon farms would have looked familiar to Vikings, so they wouldn't need to adapt what they knew from home too dramatically, although there were some technological changes coming in. The Saxons generally preferred growing crops to raising livestock; they grew wheat, barley, rye, oats, hemp, and flax. They also grew peas, cabbages, parsnips, carrots, and celery and ate fruit such as apples, blackberries, raspberries, and probably sloes (the fruit of the blackthorn). Domestic animals included goats, cattle, and sheep. Both milk and eggs were available seasonally.

The main difference for a Viking hoping to settle and farm in England was social. The early ninth century was a period of economic change. Landlords were now demanding "rents" from farmers, usually paid as foodstuffs. These Vikings effectively rent the land from the king and have yearly duties to

him—money (or goods) for the land as well as church dues and alms. They might also be expected to help build and maintain fences and fortifications, provide transport, and perform sundry other duties.

All these rents meant the intensity of agriculture needed to be increased; this led to the development of the heavy plow. These plows had a mold board that turned the soil over rather than just scratching it, bringing more nutrients to the surface. The heavy plows also needed different handling. They might need up to eight oxen to pull them, so fields became divided into the familiar medieval long strips—usually two in use and one fallow at any one time.

An increasingly sophisticated state and improved agriculture meant there was sometimes a surplus, and so markets start appearing again. These markets and fairs bring in foreign traded goods such as German quern stones, Rhenish glassware, and wheel-thrown pottery. Of course, Viking traders were probably more used to imports than Saxons anyway, but the growing idea of production that goes beyond subsistence was fairly new.

ABOVE: The Anglo-Saxons believed the arrival of the Vikings was a punishment sent from God.
FOLLOWING SPREAD: The court of Charles the Bald (Lothaire Bluteau) meets in Paris.

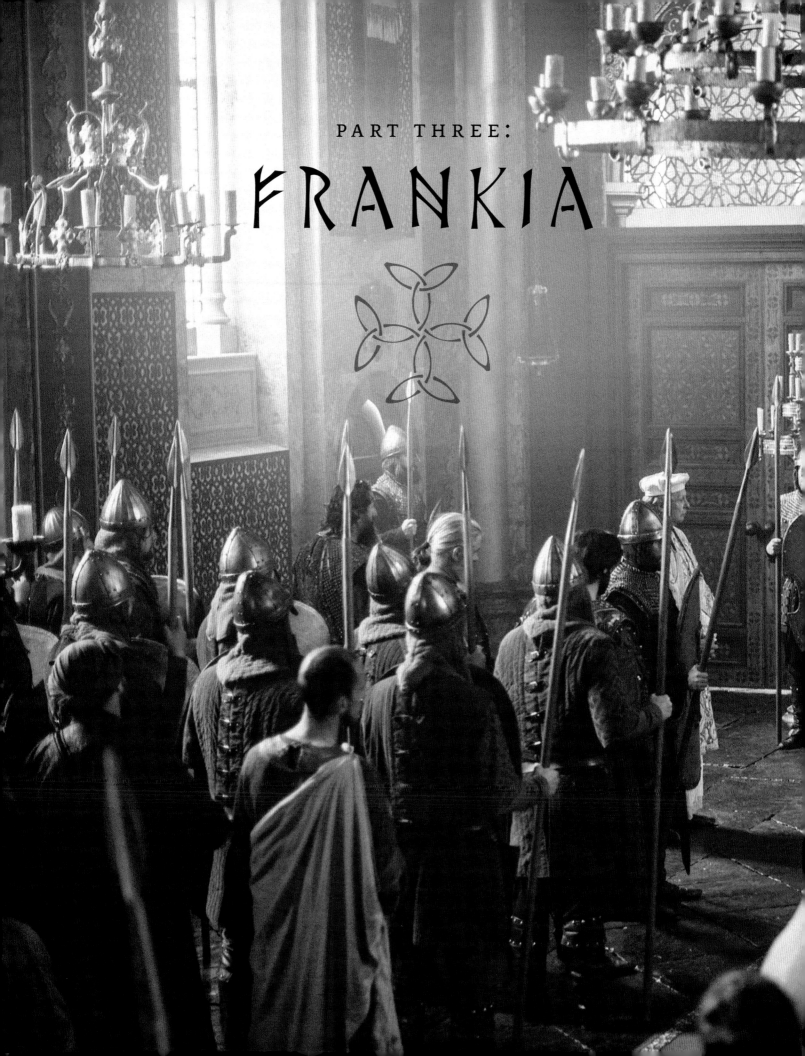

PART THREE:

FRANKIA

CAROLINGIAN FRANKIA

 ea, kings may rule over many peoples, yet they do not rule all those that they would wish to rule, but are miserable in their mind because they cannot come by all they would have . . . it was for this that a king who in old times unjustly seized the kingdom said, "Oh, how happy the man over whose head no naked sword hangs by a fine thread, as it has ever been hanging over mine!"
— BOETHIUS, *THE CONSOLATION OF PHILOSOPHY*

AT THE TIME THE VIKINGS BEGAN RAIDING IN EUROPE, there was no such country as France. Instead, what is now France was one part of the great Carolingian Empire that would reach its apogee under Charlemagne, who was crowned Holy Roman Emperor by Pope Leo III on Christmas Day, AD 800. This, in effect, made Charlemagne the legitimate successor to the Roman emperors who had once ruled much of Europe.

At its height, the Carolingian Empire was vast, stretching from the Pyrenees across all of France (except Brittany), Belgium, the Netherlands, Northern Italy, Austria, and Germany right up to the borders with modern-day Denmark. It had been founded by Charles Martel, who, though never claiming the title of king for himself, had ensured his sons became kings and his grandson an emperor. Under Charlemagne, the empire reached its zenith both in physical size and in its cultural achievements. The Carolingians modeled themselves on the Roman emperors, the remains of whose palaces, roads, and fortifications still littered their lands. This encouraged a reawakening of interest in the visual arts and literature, with Charlemagne able to attract the greatest scholars in Europe to his court. Art, literature, and music all flourished, as did trade, and many a wealthy foreign prince or would-be-king came to Charlemagne's court in search of shelter and support against enemies at home, one of those being the young Ecbert of Wessex.

The homes of the Carolingian monarchs were magnificent. The palace at Verberie-sur-Oise, a favorite of Charles the Bald, had a scale and grandeur far beyond the comprehension of most Vikings, or indeed Anglo-Saxons. It was built by Charlemagne where the Forest of Compiègne runs down to the banks of the river Oise and was approached through acres of terraced gardens, crisscrossed with canals and studded with lakes. The building itself stretched nearly five hundred yards, protected on all sides by round stone towers, its walls carved with bas-reliefs and its pediments topped with huge statues. Inside, Charles the Bald's guests walked on marble mosaics and rested on gilded furniture.

What is harder to see was how this "renaissance" affected the ordinary people of the empire beyond the frescoed walls of the palaces. Certainly the emperor improved commerce by standardizing the currency and creating a coast guard service and channel fleet to protect traders against piracy and the earliest Viking raids. He had also codified the many local laws of his empire and appointed officials from different regions to monitor regional lords to ensure that they remained loyal and applied the law fairly. Those lords consisted of around three hundred imperial officials known as "counts," each of whom administered one of the counties into which the empire was divided.

However, if Charlemagne ruled a "Roman Empire" in name, it was not an empire a Roman emperor would have recognized. City life as Romans understood it had all but ceased in the centuries following the collapse of their rule. There were still towns and markets, but these were not the major urban centers of late antiquity; but rather, smaller fortified enclosures often close to religious or administrative buildings. None of these "cities" was the capital of the empire—the emperor didn't have the administrative facilities to rule from a single place but instead was forced to permanently tour his lands, carrying justice and obedience to each area in turn. Even Paris had a population of perhaps only twenty thousand people, fewer than that of a small town today and, according to a report from the year 885, could call on just two hundred men-at-arms to defend the town should a Viking attack come. Trade between these settlements was also a shadow of its former self. The great commerce routes of Roman antiquity, based around the Mediterranean Sea, were no more than a fading memory, and what little foreign exchange existed was centered on Britain and, ironically, southern Scandinavia.

Beyond these walls the majority of the empire was rural in character, consisting of peasants settled on small farms. There were some signs of improvement in the fields where the new heavy plows and the introduction of three-field crop rotation were improving the food supply. Still, the life of the average farmer remained as precarious for the subjects of the empire as it was for the Anglo-Saxons or Vikings. Beyond the fields, the countryside was a dangerous place—as the many pilgrims who trod the roads to Rome could tell you. In addition to the bears and wolves, the countryside was full of bandits happy to cut a traveler's throat for a coin or two before slipping back into dense forests far beyond the control of the Carolingian court.

Nor was life simple for those who ruled. Carolingian custom ruled that a father's inheritance should be divided among his sons. On the death of Charlemagne, his throne had eventually passed to his sole surviving son, Louis the Pious, but his four sons fought both him and each other to become "first among equals." Theirs would prove a bitter struggle, pitting brother against brother and squandering the resources of the empire their grandfather had forged. Into these gaping dynastic wounds the Vikings crept, always willing to side with one faction against another and happy to profit from both. Within a century, the Carolingian Empire would be divided forever.

CHAPTER
11

THE HUNTERS

RAGNAR ON ARMING FOR BATTLE:

IT IS THE FATE OF NORTHMEN who cross the sea to always fight, not because we love death but because we love life. From childhood, we learn the sayings of the High One, the words of Odin himself, who warns us that for every hall we enter we should look both inside and out for "no matter where you are, you may find a foe."

It is for this reason that we learn the ways of war from the very start and arm ourselves always. A Northman's armor and weapons are his friends. They speak to his comrades of his victories, flashing gold and silver in the firelight, bringing admiration and respect, and they stand as a fearsome wall against his enemies.

Chief among the Northman's friends is his spear. It is the ash spear that stabs at close quarter and rains downs at a distance. I have seen men who can throw one in each hand both together. Even the poor hearth man can bring a spear to battle, along with the farmer's ax and the hunter's knife and bow. The tools of peace can easily be turned to weapons of war.

But no true warrior is dressed without his sword, light and flexible, whose patterned blade is a wonder of the blacksmith's art and whose pommel shines with gold. The sword is the warrior's true companion, and we give them names like "war flame," "life taker," and "truce breaker."

It is each man's duty to protect himself as well with a lime-wood shield, bound in leather and set with a central iron boss, then brightly painted as he wishes. Some wear reindeer skins that can also turn a spear away and others an iron cap. It is for each man to protect himself as best he can. The warrior, brave in battle, sports a more terrible garb, glowering out from the faceplate of his helmet and jangling in his mail coat. His wealth is plain for all to see.

But the weapon does not make the war. Let me tell you now of the way we fight. The Christians fight on the open plain and continue even when all is lost, for they believe their god will protect them. That is not our way. It is better to strike fast and be back in our ships before the enemy can muster. When we must camp, we stay close to our ships, digging a rampart around them. If we are surprised, our first thought is to run. Then we live to fight another day when the Norns may decree us better fortune.

When we must fight, we draw ourselves up in a shield wall, each shield overlapped with its neighbor. It is the honor of the youngest men to form the front row and prove themselves to their elders. Then one of our men hurls a spear over the enemy, dedicating it to Odin, whose spear throw starts every war, and battle begins. First the bowmen and the spear throwers take their part as the shield walls close in. Then the two walls probe and test each other with spears and swords. But a shield cannot pierce a shield, so we call on twenty or more men to gather into the boar formation, which we call the *svinfylking*. The *svinfylking* is a wedge of men, its point facing the enemy. It rushes forward like a giant's spear, breaking their shield wall. Then the battle is ours. It is glorious to defeat the enemy and live to fight again, and we do not seek death, but we do not fear it either. The man who dies at home will reside in Hel. The warrior struck down in battle will be taken up by the Valkyries and spend the rest of time feasting with Odin in Valhalla. Every warrior dreams of dying in battle.

DIFFERENT TONGUES
Season 1, Episode 3: "Dispossessed"

Europe in the ninth century was a place of many cultures and many languages and, while some did travel extensively, for most people much of what lay beyond their own shores was alien. We highlight this early in Season 1, where a tense standoff between King Aelle's official and Ragnar's men is intensified by the language barrier between them.

This was our first opportunity to work extensive original language into the scripts for *Vikings*. Our repertoire now includes dialogue in Old Norse, Anglo-Saxon, Old French, Old Low Franconian, and even Proto-Latgalian. Behind the scenes, a team of linguists including Erika Sigurdson (Old Norse), Kate Wiles (Anglo-Saxon), and Jim Simpson (Old French) has worked translating dialogue into languages that in some cases haven't been spoken for over a thousand years. Poll Moussoulides has then taken on the unusual dialogue-coaching job of training the cast to speak in these long-dead languages.

POLL MOUSSOULIDES (DIALOGUE COACH): This was the first time that a meaningful exchange of dialogue happened between the two cultures, and the result was electric. Several of our principal cast were going to be speaking Old Norse for the first time, and, additionally, Ragnar was going to use a smattering of Anglo-Saxon words he had picked up from Athelstan to engage the Saxons. We shot on a beautiful and secluded Irish beach, but with noisy waves in the background it was almost impossible for the actors to hear their cues. I ended up crouching behind the cameras coordinating and waving at actors when it was their turn to speak. In an unexpected way, this extra stress added to the energy of the scene as the cast were on their toes keeping all their senses active and contributing to this supercharged exchange of words.

TRAVIS FIMMEL (RAGNAR LOTHBROK): I would, hands down, be the worst on set with the languages. I have enough trouble remembering the English lines. I have to fix all my stuff in post when it comes to Saxon and Old Norse. Hirst knows this and tries not to give me much, thank the gods.

CLIVE STANDEN (ROLLO): When we first got together with Poll, our dialect coach, and he started working through the old Norse dialogue, it was strikingly hard to get to grips with. It felt like learning Klingon. Three years and three seasons later, I can now quickly decipher what each sentence and word means and have found myself being able to roughly translate other people's Norse dialogue into English as I hear

it. I can safely say I speak more Old Norse now than any of the French I learned at school, a daunting thought going into Season 4, playing the future Duke of Normandy!

LINUS ROACHE (KING ECBERT): On one occasion, I was asked to add a line of Anglo-Saxon dialogue the night before shooting a scene. This resulted in my jumping off a cart, going completely blank on the line, and then turning to Katheryn and just saying some gobbledygook like, "Watcha Ma Hunga Zunga." Katheryn and George, being total professionals and not wanting to waste the shot, just looked at me and carried on with their dialogue as if nothing weird had happened at all.

KEN GIROTTI (DIRECTOR): Michael Hirst almost always chooses a language to base a scene around, and it's not always Old Norse. In cases like that, one side speaks in the ancient language and whoever's point of view we happen to be in with the scene speaks English. But in rare cases we've had all characters speaking in foreign tongues, and that's fun. It can be a great vehicle for comedy as well. That's when I think it really works.

JEFF WOOLNOUGH (DIRECTOR): At the end of the Mercian battle, Burgred surrenders in Anglo-Saxon, pleading with Ragnar and Athelwulf: "Don't quelch meh." "Quelch" is a better word for "kill," isn't it? I think we should lobby for it to be returned to modern English. The fun part about portraying the old languages is discovering the roots of the words we use today.

PREVIOUS SPREAD: Ragnar pauses in his battle with the Franks.

SWEARING IN OLD NORSE

The use of original languages throughout the series is one of the defining features of *Vikings*. But beyond the Old Norse dialogue, the language team also tried to provide the cast with the day-to-day phrases, jibes, and swear words that we hear fleetingly in battle scenes and at feasts, and which provide an authentically coarse soundtrack to the series.

Some of the historically accurate phrases we've used include:

Þú berjast sem kelling.	You fight like an old woman.
Þú ert tannber og tannljótr, úteygðr og munnviðr.	You have ugly, sticking-out teeth, bug eyes, and a wide mouth.
Hann var húskarl og heldur ógæfur og vinnulítil.	He was a servant, and rather stubborn and lazy.
Kerlingar nef.	Old-woman nose. [Nickname.]
Það þykir mér fádæmi hversu lítt þú ert vaxinn niður!	It seems remarkable to me how small you are down there!
Miður hæddu konur að okkur, þá er við vorum yngri.	Women laughed at us less when we were younger.
Þá var dregin burst úr nefi þér.	Then a bristle was dragged from your nose. [i.e., you were cheated.]
Þeim mun í brún bregða ok ofarliga klæja.	Their eyebrows will twitch, and their upper part will itch.
Slíkt kalla eg argaskatt.	I call such as this a shit-tax. [In response to bad goods. *Argr* also has sexual connotations.]
Mogaðu kellingu sjúka!	Go bang a sick old lady!
Þú kannt at láta freti fjúka.	You know how to let fly a fart.
þat þikkir þér sómi, at serða páfann at Rómi.	It seems to you an honor to fuck the pope in Rome. [This is from an actual medieval poem.]
Þú núir snjóta en serður ábóta.	You rub nobs and fuck abbots.
streður hann þat er kvikt er flest.	He screws most things that are alive.

VIKING CAMP
Season 3, Episode 7: "Paris"

In Season 3, Episode 7, we get to see a full Viking war camp under construction as Ragnar and his men dig in for the siege of Paris. Viking war bands went to great lengths to build and defend their camps, paying particular attention to the need to defend their ships and provide themselves with a quick escape route if necessary. Archaeological and historical information provided the crew with details to help bring these camps alive. We know from excavations at Repton in England that plagues could break out in the confined quarters of winter camps, as indicated by the 249 Viking skeletons found in a reused chapel there.

Thanks to the contemporary Abbo the Crooked we even have a physical description of the camps built of stakes and stones and earth—so probably consisting of an enclosure with tents and huts surrounded by a ditch and bank with a wooden palisade. This was one of the rare occasions when we have a firsthand description to base our set on. We also know that these camps could be chaotic—filled with rustled animals, stolen food, booty from raids, and all the paraphernalia of war—the axes, spears, bows, and, most important, the individual warriors' shields.

We also needed to populate this camp in an interesting and authentic way. The *Anglo-Saxon Chronicle* describes one Viking camp in England being overrun by the English who capture women and children, suggesting that these camps were by no means male-only preserves. This provided another chance to put women in scenes that movies have traditionally made all male.

JIL TURNER (SET DECORATOR): I knew how important the Viking shields were, and I was desperate to get it right. I settled on a thirty-inch round, planked shield with various metalwork around the rim and across the front. To show that they had been in battle before, I had metalwork attached randomly, as if they had been repaired after each battle by its owner.

Then there was the question of colors and designs for each shield. Each of the 250 raiders' shields is unique, painted in different colors, patterns, and motifs. We also had certain characters linked. In the first few episodes, Ragnar had a teal-blue shield with a small arrowhead painted on it. His brother Rollo had a shield in the same color but with an orange X across it, but also with the arrow motif. Lagertha, Ragnar's wife and a shield maiden, has a shield in the same color with a subtle tracery design around the central boss. This way they were all slightly different, but by keeping them in the same basic color, it subliminally told the audience that they were family.

OPPOSITE: Lagertha leads her warriors in the assault on Paris.

CHAPTER
12
THE HUNTED

CHARLES THE BALD ON THE CHRISTIAN WORLD:

LET ME TELL YOU OF THE WORLD where Christ still rules. At the center of everything lies the Holy City of Jerusalem, around which are the places of the Bible—although these lands have since been overrun by the Saracens. Brave is the pilgrim who sets out for the middle of the world.

On the edge of the Holy Lands lies Constantinople, the city built by Constantine who made the whole Roman world Christian. It was here that the emperor moved his court from Rome and here today a part of that empire clings on.

The other part, that of the West, is my inheritance. When the Holy Father made my grandfather emperor of the Romans, my family took on the Roman mantle blessed by the successor to St. Peter himself who holds the keys to the gate of heaven.

But what of the people of the empire? When the age of the Caesars ended, it was my people, the Franks, who settled in what had been Gaul, making it our kingdom, and we remain there still, though our rule has spread far beyond. Mine is the mightiest of Christian empires, stretching from the Spanish borders to Saxony and the land of the Lombards. It is to me that the Holy Father looks for his safety.

But the land of the Franks is very wide and wild, and, though cities have sprung up, they are not as they were in former times, for many are small and mean. For the most part, the people live in villages, and, beyond these, and around them, lie the forests, which are dark and deep and full of wild animals. On the roads there are many bandits, and the seas are full of pirates. It is my struggle to return this land to happier days.

Across the waters to the west lie the Christian English, who have seven petty kingdoms—Northumbria, Mercia, East Anglia, Essex, Kent, Sussex, and Wessex—and more smaller ones besides. These are surrounded by ancient places where the people of older times were driven when the Romans left. They are the lands of the foreigners they call "Welsh" and the "West Welsh," who some call "Cornish", and to the north are the Scots and Picts. Across the sea lies the land of the Irish.

To the south of Frankia lies the Roman Sea, although today it is home to Saracen fleets that prowl the waters and take unwary Christians for their slaves. The Saracens moved out from their homelands many centuries ago and now occupy all north Africa and Iberia.

And then there is the north. Across the great earthwork that they call the Danevirke lie the lands of the Northmen. Few Christians would travel there, in pagan places where they sacrifice people to their false gods. They live protected by their wild land, full of cold lakes and impassable mountains, and from this fortress they venture out to bring death to the Christians. They are a scourge sent by God.

They sit beyond the grace of God, in the wastelands at the edge of the world, and what lies beyond that, no man can tell.

THE STORY OF
CHARLES THE BALD

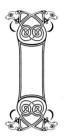

Charles the Bald is the emperor of the western part of the much vaster empire carved out by his famous grandfather, Charlemagne. With his capital at the Roman-built city of Paris, Charles becomes very vulnerable to the raiding parties emerging from Scandinavia. Like many rulers, Charles dithers—not knowing whether to try and buy the Vikings off, or fight them. His solution is somewhat unexpected.

–Michael Hirst

Charles the Bald was king of West Frankia, king of Italy, and eventually became the Holy Roman Emperor. Charles's father had been the widely admired Louis the Pious, the son of Charlemagne, but Charles's birth to Louis's second wife, Judith of Bavaria, created a split in the empire. Louis had already allocated subkingdoms to his other sons but when little Charles was born to a new wife, he tried to give Charles a kingdom too—and this kicked off three civil wars. After the wars, Charles succeeded in acquiring the western third of the Carolingian Empire, making him probably the most successful of Louis's sons.

For his day, Charles was a highly educated man of letters. He relied on the church rather than his nobles to provide administrators to run his country. He was a practical and relatively enlightened ruler, a true heir to Charlemagne, who was unable to bring about another Carolingian renaissance, due mainly to the faithlessness of his own family. Even so, compared to Wessex, or anywhere in Scandinavia, Charles's court was utterly glittering.

Charles suffered a miserable end. Archbishop Hincmar relates how Charles, suffering from a fever, was persuaded by his doctor to drink a powder that was poisoned; some eleven days later, it led to his death "in a wretched little hut." This was not an end to the emperor's ignominy, however. He had died in a mountain refuge in the Alps, a very long way from the royal church of St. Denis, and so:

"His attendants opened him up, took out his intestines, poured in such wine and aromatics as they had, put the body on a bier and set off to carry him to St. Denis."

Sadly, his sudden death had taken them all by surprise and their preparations for the body proved insufficient, as Hincmar explains:

"Because of the stench they could carry him no further; so they put him in a barrel, which they smeared with pitch inside and outside and encased in hides, but even this did nothing to get rid of the smell. Only with difficulty did they manage to reach Nantua, a little monastery in the archdiocese of Lyons, and there they committed the body, with its barrel, to the earth."

So the emperor of the Franks was buried in a tarred barrel in a little-known monastery. It was many years before anyone had the courage to dig up this hideous package and transfer his remains to Paris.

LOTHAIRE BLUETEAU (CHARLES THE BALD): On our first meeting, Michael Hirst talked of the last czar of Russia. From that I knew where to search to find Charles the Bald. Michael starts with historical facts and plays with dates, then amalgamates a few historical figures into one. So I did the same. I read everything on the lineage of Carolingian figures, along with personal details. I borrowed his stutter from his child Louis the Stammerer because I felt it fitted with his lack of confidence coming from such an inheritance and his struggle against his brothers.

I wanted to offer an emperor that would bring a different light to a triumvirate—Ragnar, so powerful and a natural leader; Ecbert, Machiavellian; and Charles, so full of doubts, low self-esteem, and temperament, faced with such an inheritance and his emotionally charged struggle against his brothers.

ABOVE: Lothaire Bluteau as Charles the Bald.
PREVIOUS SPREAD: Europe at the time of the Viking invasions.

CHAPTER 12: THE HUNTED 143

DESIGNING PARIS

Paris in the year 845 was a city in what was then West Frankia. Having said that, it wasn't much of a city, more a conglomeration of villages on a natural island, the Île de la Cité, connected to the shore by two wooden bridges. The city had once been the much larger, Roman center of Lutetia, but it had fallen on hard times.

After the collapse of Roman rule, the Merovingian monarchs of Frankia made Paris their capital and the Abbey of St. Denis the burial place of their rulers, as it remained for all but three of the kings of France. Under the Carolingians, however, its fortunes had faltered. With greater imperial ambitions, Carolingian kings were always away on campaign, and when the empire reached its height, Charlemagne found Aix-la-Chapelle (Aachen) a more convenient and central location from which to rule. Removed from the center of power, Paris fell under the control of the counts of Paris, becoming little more than a regional center.

However, by the standards of the day, Paris was an impressive sight for any Viking and it is here that our heroes come face-to-face with those who claimed to be the successors to the Roman empire—the Carolingian emperors. As a set, then, this had to be a distinctive "third look," different from Viking Kattegat or Anglo-Saxon England. It was also a daunting prospect—re-creating an island city that hadn't been seen for a thousand years.

P.J. DILLON (DIRECTOR OF PHOTOGRAPHY): We have used color to differentiate among Scandinavia (Kattegat and Hedeby), England (Wessex and Mercia), and France (Paris). Scandinavia tends to have colder tones, less saturation, and is a little more contrast-y than England, which has richer greens and generally more saturation. The contrast levels also tend to be a little less in England. Paris is different again; it is more saturated than England or Scandinavia, and the production design and costumes have a richer color palette with more primary reds, yellows, and blues—tones that are not really used in Scandinavia.

JIL TURNER (SET DECORATOR): The production designer had wanted Paris to seem much more colorful and advanced than Scandinavia. To achieve this, I made a lot of the set dressing richer and a lot more ornate. I had a beautiful twelve-foot table made with a delicate inlay for the French king's antechamber. To accompany this, I also had twelve Roman-style chairs made as well. These gave an impression of order and wealth that would fit a great king. The runner stretching up to the golden throne was sixty-six feet long. On either side of his throne I placed two carved unicorns. On either side of those were two brass candelabras.

DOMINIC REMANE (VISUAL EFFECTS SUPERVISOR): The siege of Paris contained 293 visual effects shots, 45 of which showcased the city of Paris in great detail. Several shots required a fully digital model of the city and surrounding landscape. From the blades of grass to the monolithic cathedral and to the digital warriors scaling the walls, Visual Effects helped bring Michael's vision of Paris to reality.

OPPOSITE TOP AND FOLLOWING SPREAD: The whole of ninth-century Paris was recreated in CGI for Season 3.
OPPOSITE BOTTOM: A nineteenth-century portrayal of a Viking siege of Paris.

THE STORY OF
PRINCESS GISLA

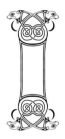

Princess Gisla is Charles the Bald's only daughter. She is actually not very impressed by her father's faint heart and lack of courage when faced with the Northmen—and even less impressed when her father forces her to marry Rollo, the great warrior, as a way of persuading him to protect Paris rather than attack it. But a new dynasty is about to be formed, which once more will change the history of the world.

—MICHAEL HIRST

For *Vikings* we condensed the history of the mid-ninth century, by making the rather shadowy figure of Princess Gisla the daughter of Charles the Bald, rather than Charles the Simple, as was probably the case. She was still, however, betrothed to Rollo, who would go on to become the first duke (or count) of Normandy in the early tenth century.

The historical Rollo had invaded the area known today as Normandy and attacked Paris before laying siege to Chartres. In the subsequent Treaty of Saint-Clair-sur-Epte with King Charles, Rollo pledged feudal allegiance to the king and converted, at least nominally, to Christianity, probably taking on the baptismal name Robert. According to the chronicler Dudo of St. Quentin in his *Historia Normannorum*, he also received the hand of Charles's daughter Gisla in marriage and was granted all the lands from the river Epte to the sea as well as parts of Brittany. He also became the ruler of Normandy as either a duke or a count.

Only Dudo mentions Gisla, so we have no independent records of her life, but French traditions say Rollo mistreated her, executing the two knights sent to protect her. She died, childless, not long after.

JOAN BERGIN (COSTUME DESIGNER): The Franks are a just reward for two years of Vikings and the sturdy re-creating of their clothed lives. Suddenly we are in gilded, jeweled, silk fabric to our ears and combined with the fabulous hand-painted interiors, stained glass in forty glorious shades, and a workshop outdoing itself to produce the zenith of a Byzantine-influenced court to compete with each sumptuous setting. All departments got on a roll, and the creative energy was contagious. The French actors added their own élan.

It was important that Gisla be seen as a princess apart. Royal to her fingertips, with a self-assured hauteur, she was as caring and brave as any of her father's entourage, but in the body of a young woman. Her costumes at times echo a touch of male intent, silk trousers peeking out from under a tunic, sweeping cloaks, and fine leather boots. Otherwise her clothes are lavish and ornate, befitting a princess of the Carolingian court.

LOTHAIRE BLUTEAU (CHARLES THE BALD): Joan Bergin is a partner not only for the design of the period but she also comes to the rehearsal every day to look at the scene and feel through the blocking what is needed. There was a scene for which my character needed a "blanket"—like a kid having a fit who wraps himself on his throne. She changed the costume on the day and rushed to serve the emotion and energy of the scene. That is rare. They were also working very tightly with the production designer and art director, not to mention hair and makeup, to use the style of the period and make it alive.

OPPOSITE: Princess Gisla (Morgane Polanski) takes the Oriflamme.

SCORING VIKING MUSIC

We know very little about Viking music, having very few examples of Viking instruments from archaeological sites and no written music. However, two Viking recorders have been found in Sweden, one four-holed example at Västerby and another with five holes in Konsterud, Värmland.

In Carolingian Frankia we know a little more, as Charlemagne was interested in music and encouraged the writing of musical treatises such as the *Musica Enchiriadis*. From his era we also get the first musical notation in Western music.

Among the Anglo-Saxons there is less evidence. We know from written sources that monks sang plainchant and that singing and harp playing were popular accompaniments to meals, but no notation from the ninth century survives to tell us what this sounded like.

With little more to go on than drawings and some later church musical notation, the challenge for *Vikings* composer Trevor Morris was to breathe life into long-silent musical instruments in a way which felt authentic to the period but was accessible to a modern audience.

TREVOR MORRIS (COMPOSER): The challenge was to make the music in *Vikings* relevant, make it "today" in some way, and yet still suit what is on screen. We've evolved the score over three seasons, to the point now where it is about 90 percent electronically driven, and it totally works. Mind you, it took me thirty episodes of scoring to find the "right" electronics.

In Season 1, the score was more driven by orchestral and string instruments.

As it progresses, the themes are more about giving the balance of power to a certain character, or backing up Ragnar, or helping tell the shifts in fortune within a long battle sequence.

The goal of the music at the end of the day is to support the story and, more important, the goal of giving us, the audience, a different and unique look and insight into this amazing culture. Pop culture surely knows only a fraction of what they were really about and what they accomplished. It's an amazing journey to go on, and the music hopefully is the magic carpet to guide us along for the ride.

KEN GIROTTI (DIRECTOR): For Viking music we also use Wardruna, a Norwegian musical group led by Einar Selvik. They use traditional Nordic instruments and poetic meters as well as lyrics written in Norwegian, Old Norse, and the Proto-Norse tongue. What a great find that was (pure dumb luck on my part). The music of this group was perfect for the feel I wanted to create at Uppsala.

OPPOSITE: Preparing the siege engines for the attack on Paris.

THE SEIGE OF PARIS

Providing the fine detail needed for the Parisian scenes in Season 3 was hindered by the very scant historical detail available for Ragnar's raid. We know that sometime in March 845, Ragnar's fleet of 120 ships, with roughly five thousand men, entered the Seine. En route to Paris, Ragnar had raided Rouen, raising the alarm with Charles—who abandoned Paris, having decided that his first duty was to protect the royal Abbey of St. Denis (near, but not in, Paris). Having raised an army (a peasant levy with a few mercenaries and lords who owed service to him), Charles recklessly decided to split his meager force in two, putting one on each bank of the river. Ragnar, very practically, decided to attack a division of the smaller of the two forces; he took 111 prisoners. With his usual aplomb, he then shipped all 111 to an island in the Seine, where he hanged the lot in full view of the other force. Frankish

sources claim this was to honor Odin, but, of course, the main reason was simply to terrify Charles's army, and it worked: They promptly deserted.

Ragnar finally arrived in Paris during Easter, and plundered it. The date was deliberate, of course—Vikings loved attacking during Christian festivals as no one was prepared, all the best silver was out, and it demonstrated the impotence of the Christian god.

Sometime during this attack, plague broke out among the Vikings. All our sources are Christian so it's difficult to know exactly what happened next, but it is claimed that Ragnar's men prayed to their gods before beginning a penitent fast on the advice of a Christian prisoner. This seemed to work, and

the plague subsided. Charles managed a scrambled defense but quickly realized that he couldn't win, so he bribed the invaders to go away with seven thousand (French) pounds of gold and silver. This was the first time *Danegeld* (a payment to Vikings to get them to leave) was paid, and it set something of a precedent. From then on, Vikings often turned up and didn't risk an actual raid but just waited to be paid off. This would happen another twelve times in Frankia.

What we needed for this series of scenes, however, was fine detail on how the siege might have played out. Sadly, there are no eyewitness records of this attack. Fortunately, another raid in 885 is recorded in some detail by Abbo the Crooked, who was a young monk at the abbey of Saint-Germain-Des-Prés near Paris. His *Bella Parisiacae Urbis* became our major source for reconstructing our ninth-century Parisian siege, offering a glimpse of what it was like to be there. By dissecting this account, we could re-create a series of authentic scenes and vignettes to use in our dramatic retelling.

Abbo describes various Viking attempts to undermine the wall of the stone tower while the Frankish defenders, just a few hundred men-at-arms at the time, tried to prevent them reaching the wall by throwing stones on them and firing *ballistae* (Roman-style large crossbows) at them. Abbo at one point claims that a "javelin" from one of these skewered seven Vikings at once. Odo, the count of Paris in charge of the defense of the city, then jokes about taking them back to the kitchen like meat on a skewer.

Abbo also records the Franks making a burning liquid comprising wax, oil, and pitch—like napalm—which they poured over the Vikings at the base of the wall. He records with some delight how the skulls of the Vikings split open when the hot oil hit them.

The Vikings themselves adopted various tactics, including setting fire to the gates, which blinded and choked the Franks. Some Franks ran to reinforce the tower, which was separate from the city, one of them carrying a rallying banner—the first time in history that the famous French sacred banner, the Oriflamme, is mentioned.

Later on, they built wooden catapults to hurl pots of molten lead (probably stolen from church roofs) into the city, as well as trying to burn the city by sailing fireships toward the main bridges, although Abbo records that winter storms did more damage than fireship attacks.

Abbo's account of the end of this siege is rather unclear. In a confused passage, a Viking standard-bearer gets killed and they seem to lose heart. One group stayed in camp while the others portaged their ships (dragging them overland) past Paris and back onto the Seine before heading for the Loire.

The remaining Vikings built a wall around Saint-Germain-Des-Prés, cutting it off, and extracted sixty pounds of silver ransom to go away. A truce was eventually called, and the Franks and Vikings agreed on peace. For *Vikings*, we would use another stratagem.

ABOVE: Lagertha takes on the Parisian men-at-arms.
OPPOSITE: Björn Ironside scales the battlements.

RAGNAR TAKES PARIS
SEASON 3, EPISODE 10: "THE DEAD"

In Season 3, Episode 10, Ragnar takes Paris by trickery. The inspiration for this episode comes from a story recounted by the chronicler Dudo of St. Quentin in his *Historia Normannorum*. In 860, after raiding down the Spanish coast and fighting their way through the Straits of Gibraltar into the Mediterranean, Björn and his brother pillaged the south of France before landing in Italy and capturing Pisa. From here they marched inland to a large city that they took to be Rome but that was, in fact, Luna. Unable to breach the defenses, they reverted to a clever stratagem. They sent the bishop of the city a message that Hastein had died but had converted to Christianity on his deathbed and asked if he could be buried in consecrated ground. The gullible bishop allowed the coffin and entourage into the city—at which point Hastein leapt up and fought his way to the gates, opening them to let his raiders in. The brothers then raided Sicily and North Africa before turning for home. At the Straits of Gibraltar they were intercepted by the Saracen navy and lost forty ships when attacked with the incendiary weapon known as "Greek Fire." The remainder of his fleet managed to return to Scandinavia.

GUSTAF SKARSGÅRD (FLOKI): My favorite scene of Season 3 was when Floki is losing it inside his burning siege tower. A beautiful monologue in Old Norse and a frantic situation with many layers. Great fun for an actor!

P.J. DILLON (DIRECTOR OF PHOTOGRAPHY): The most complex scene we've had to shoot must be the attack on Paris from Season 3. We shot over several weeks on several different locations and sets (some involving battle sequences on a platform more than thirty feet off the ground!), massive amounts of green screen, and ever-changing weather!

BILL HALLIDAY (VFX PRODUCER): The plan was to reference the existing cities of Carcassonne for the exterior walls and Mont. St. Michel for the interior city. The walls of Carcassonne were accurate to the time but most of Mont St. Michel was several hundred years too new and built on a much higher elevation than Île de la Cité, which was the site of ninth-century Paris. Dominic Remane (VFX supervisor) and Mark Geraghty (production designer) traveled to Carcassonne at one point to conduct a photographic survey of the walls, battlements, and towers. The photographs were eventually used to create the textures for the digital model.

For the siege we did a lot of "gore augmentation"—effectively, adding blood and wounds digitally. There are several methods we employ to add the gore, but usually it involves using an element of blood spray or splatter that would have been shot against a green screen. Selecting the green, then removing the color (a method known as "keying") leaves us with only the blood element. This later gets tracked to the performers' bodies and integrated into the shot. In some instances, we would need to create the blood entirely within the computer. This is the more complex solution and can require a great deal of computational power to simulate the real-world elements such as gravity and viscosity.

OPPOSITE: Ragnar outmaneuvers King Charles.
PREVIOUS SPREAD: The walls of Paris reconstructed in studio for the stunt teams.

Visual Effects tends to be heavily relied upon in battle sequences. Some of the typical things we would do in addition to gore augmentation would be adding digital arrows, cross-bow bolts, increasing the size of crowds, enhancing the size and intensity of fires and extending sets. All of these effects factor heavily in our Siege of Paris this season.

FRANKIE MCCAFFERTY (SINRIC): I think one of the funniest nights I had was shooting the attack on Paris where hordes of us storm across a bridge. The wisecracks and quips were coming thick and fast, and at one point all the supporting artists spontaneously began singing the theme from the 1980s TV show *Cheers*. A bunch of bare-chested, tattooed berserkers singing "You wanna be where everybody knows your name!" is one of the most surreal things I have ever witnessed.

ABOVE: Princess Gisla is held to ransom.
OPPOSITE: *Vikings* creator Michael Hirst with director Ken Girotti.

ΛFTERWORD: THE FRΛNKS

By Michael Hirst

DURING MY INITIAL RESEARCH INTO THE VIKINGS, their history and their travels, I had of course come across descriptions of their famous raid on Paris in 885, and the subsequent siege of the city. The sheer scale and ambition of the raid—reputedly a hundred ships and around 3,000 warriors—was itself exciting, but at the time I felt certain that it would be too big an undertaking for our show. We were starting, after all, in a small Viking settlement, and featuring a farmer, his wife and children, and the first raid involved about thirty warriors in a single ship attacking a solitary English monastery.

How to go from there, in two seasons, to such a spectacular and almost jaw-dropping event as the siege of Paris?

I continued to ponder this, even as our own production grew bigger, bolder, and more ambitious. With larger "armies" our Vikings successfully raided English towns and kingdoms. We were continuously stepping-up and I began to feel that this trajectory, reflecting as it did the actual historical narrative of Viking expansionism in the 8th and 9th centuries, had to be continued.

At the same time I was also aware of the rapid developments in CGI—visual effects—that would help us to create the sheer scale of the attack, and the furious attempts by the Franks to repulse it. Now, it's always been something I'm very proud of, that unlike many other shows and indeed movies, *Vikings* doesn't depend for its drama on computerized visual effects. It's a show about real people and real events, and it is shot for

real. Our actors, male and female, actually fight. They sail boats, they ride horses, they use weapons, they get bruised. I knew they would still have to be as physical and as "present" if we raided Paris, but this time I knew we would need the additional benefits that CGI can bring.

And there was another issue. By featuring Paris in the third season of the show I was bringing the event forward in time. I confess it. I hold my hands up. I used the liberties of poetic license to place the siege of Paris into my saga of Ragnar Lothbrok. Why? Well, the truth is you never know what is going to happen in the world of TV drama. Even good shows get arbitrarily cancelled. And although I believed that the History Channel would continue to support and sustain us, I could not take the slightest chance that we would miss out in recreating one of—for me—the most compelling and awesome events of the Dark Ages.

There was another reason, closer as it were to home. A drama series as challenging as *Vikings* needs to be refreshed from time to time. That might mean bringing on new characters, or running new and unexpected story lines. Or, in this case, it might mean creating a new world. I had seen later woodcuts of the siege which showed hundreds of ladders up against the walls of Paris, and thousands of Viking attackers swarming up them. There were piles of dead, jostling lines of ships; some of the ladders were on fire and flaming bodies were falling out the sky like Icarus.

I gave these images to our production designer, Mark Geraghty and, as I had anticipated, they set off explosions in his mind. Here, indeed, was a new world to discover and reinvent, and on a new scale. Roman Paris! With its bridges, battlements, towers; the Cathedral of Notre Dame; its narrow, teeming streets of brick and stone. Soon, Mark and his team were building the interior of the Cathedral on one of our sound stages—the biggest build we had attempted so far. The Cathedral glows with light from a thousand candles at night, and in the daytime the sunlight makes the stained glass window glow with brilliant colors, which stain the marble columns and floor.

And if Mark was excited to start work on his ambitious designs and builds, so was our famous costume designer, Joan Bergin, to start creating a Frankish wardrobe. Restrained, for a couple of seasons, by the earthy hues of Viking and Saxon costume—though never defeated by them—Joan now had a richer, more cultivated, more flamboyant cast to dress and shape. The results are spectacular, as I knew they would be.

Indeed, walking around the new sets, and round the backlot on which we were also building a section of the walls of Paris, and one of the bridges leading into the city, I could feel strongly the general excitement. We are blessed with a very committed and happy crew in Ireland, but even they appreciate turning their hands and brains to new and fresh challenges.

Then of course we had new cast, playing the Emperor Charles the Bald, his daughter Princess Gisla, and Count Odo, the military commander of the city with his famous iron hand. Their arrival put everyone on note, although naturally our established players, like Travis, Kathryn, Clive, and Alexander, were themselves already enthused by the idea of engaging in a new kind of warfare in a very different landscape.

It was never going to be easy to shoot on this scale, and it's to his great credit that our Canadian director at the time, Kelly Makin, found ways and means to overcome or negotiate the many obstacles that confronted the production. And yet it was still fun, for the most part, because creativity is supposed to be fun. Everyone was being stretched to the limits of their capabilities, but that's how it should be; because everyone was working towards achieving something they all believed in.

During this time, I was visited by an old friend, a Professor of Economics, and his new American girlfriend. I warned them that watching a show being filmed is like watching paint dry: it takes a lot of coats and it's agonizingly slow.

We walked out onto the backlot. We were shooting with two crews that day, working on different scenes. When we reached the walls we saw hundreds of extras and dozens of stunt men and women climbing up ramps and ladders trying to reach the battlements. Crossbow bolts were fizzing all around them. Then the ladders were set on fire. The stunt warriors and shield-maidens, suddenly alight, fell, some of them from the very top of the ladders, into about eight feet of water. When they got out, they did the whole thing again.

Meanwhile we moved on to the bridge. There, covered by a shield of animal hides, Viking attackers were using a battering ram to try and break down the doors of Paris whilst, from above, Frankish defenders fired bolts, threw huge boulders, and rained fire down upon them.

The Professor of Economics said he had never watched paint drying in such a dramatic way, and would henceforth take everything I told him about the world of filmmaking with a large pinch of salt. He did make the point that I was being paid it seemed to live in a world of fantasy, but I countered by saying that was surely also true of him!

I sometimes reflect that I do what I do—write drama based upon historical material—because I feel excited to enter and explore other worlds. And then somehow to connect these past worlds and people to our own world and to ourselves. Taking my story into Paris, into a world actually foreign to contemporary Parisians, was an adventure but also an education. I wouldn't have missed it for the world.

And it is my dream and aspiration to take my beloved Vikings on into yet more fantastic and unexpected worlds: to Spain, Iceland, Greenland and yes, finally, to the shores of North America.